CEH™ v11
Certified Ethical Hacker
Version 11
Practice Tests
Second Edition

T0254089

Ric Messier

SYBEX®
A Wiley Brand

For my best friend, partner, and the best support and cheerleader I could ask for, Robin.

Acknowledgments

Thanks to my agent, Carole, for always looking out for me, and thanks to Robin for always supporting me and keeping me going as I worked through this process. Thanks as well to the Wiley staff, Tom Dinse, and Jim Minatel for their support through the editing of this book.

The publisher wishes to acknowledge the work of Raymond Blockmon, the author of the previous Sybex book *CEH v9: Certified Ethical Hacker Version 9 Practice Tests*. Although this new book, *CEH v11: Certified Ethical Hacker Version 11 Practice Tests*, is heavily updated with new and revised questions, Raymond's work on the CEH v9 book laid the foundation that made this new CEH v11 book possible.

About the Author

Ric Messier got started in information security in the early 1980s by discovering a privilege escalation vulnerability on an IBM mainframe that opened the door to the worldwide network of the BITNET for him. Since that time, he has been a programmer, system administrator, network engineer, security consultant, instructor, program director, and penetration tester as well as having led a security engineering team at a global Internet service provider (the company that built the ARPAnet). He has developed many training courses as well as having developed graduate degree programs for two colleges. Additionally, he's taught courses at Brandeis University, Champlain College, University of Colorado at Boulder, and Harvard University. He holds CEH, CCSP, GCIH, GSEC, and CISSP certifications and has previously held CCNA, MCSE, and MCP+I certifications. Additionally, he has a Master of Science degree in Digital forensic science. He is currently a Principal Consultant with Mandiant, a world leader in incident response and security consulting.

About the Technical Editor

Kenneth Tanner is an IT professional with 25+ years of extensive hands-on experience in networking, telecommunications, and systems administration, and the security thereof. He is currently a Senior Technical Instructor at FireEye/Mandiant where he provides instruction on incident response. He has also worked for Hughes Training, The University of Alabama System, and various private companies as a consultant and/or instructor. Kenneth attended the University of Alabama at Birmingham (UAB) in Birmingham, Alabama where he received both a Bachelor and Master of Science degree in Electrical Engineering. He currently holds the following certifications: (ISC)² CISSP, EC-Council CEH, CND and CHFI, CompTIA CASP, PenTest+, CySA+, Security+, and Network+, Cisco CCNA Route and Switch, CCNA Security, CCNA Voice, CCNA CyberOps, and CCDA, Axelos ITIL, Metasploit Pro Certified Specialist, and Nexpose Certified Administrator. He has taught many of the certifications he holds. Kenneth lives in Colorado with his wife, Nadean, and their two children Shelby and Gavin.

Contents

Introduction

This exam book is designed to give the CEH candidate a realistic idea of what the CEH exam will look like. As a candidate, you should be familiar with Wireshark, Nmap, and other tools. To get the most out of these exams, you should consider constructing a virtual lab and practicing with the tools to become familiar with viewing the logs that are generated. In preparing for the CEH exam, you will benefit greatly by using YouTube. YouTube is a goldmine of information—and it's free. It is also recommended that you keep up with the latest malware and cybersecurity news provided online. Most cybersecurity-related websites provide insight on the latest vulnerabilities and exploits that are in the wild. Keeping up-to-date with this information will only add value to your CEH knowledge and will help solidify your understanding even more.

What Is a CEH?

The Certified Ethical Hacker exam is to validate that those holding the certification understand the broad range of subject matter that is required for someone to be an effective ethical hacker. The reality is that most days, if you are paying attention to the news, you will see a news story about a company that has been compromised and had data stolen, a government that has been attacked, or even enormous denial-of-service attacks, making it difficult for users to gain access to business resources.

The CEH is a certification that recognizes the importance of identifying security issues to get them remediated. This is one way companies can protect themselves against attacks—by getting there before the attackers do. It requires someone who knows how to follow techniques that attackers would normally use. Just running scans using automated tools is insufficient because as good as security scanners may be, they will identify false positives—cases where the scanner indicates an issue that isn't really an issue. Additionally, they will miss a lot of vulnerabilities—false negatives—for a variety of reasons, including the fact that the vulnerability or attack may not be known.

Because companies need to understand where they are vulnerable to attack, they need people who are able to identify those vulnerabilities, which can be very complex. Scanners are a good start, but being able to find holes in complex networks can take the creative intelligence that humans offer. This is why we need ethical hackers. These are people who can take extensive knowledge of a broad range of technical subjects and use it to identify vulnerabilities that can be exploited.

The important part of that two-word phrase, by the way, is "ethical." Companies have protections in place because they have resources they don't want stolen or damaged. When they bring in someone who is looking for vulnerabilities to exploit, they need to be certain that nothing will be stolen or damaged. They also need to be certain that anything that may be seen or reviewed isn't shared with anyone else. This is especially true when it comes to any vulnerabilities that have been identified.

The CEH exam, then, has a dual purpose. It not only tests deeply technical knowledge but also binds anyone who is a certification holder to a code of conduct. Not only will you be expected to know the content and expectations of that code of conduct, you will be expected to live by that code. When companies hire or contract to people who have their CEH certification, they can be assured they have brought on someone with discretion who can keep their secrets and provide them with professional service in order to help improve their security posture and keep their important resources protected.

About the Exam

The CEH exam has much the same parameters as other professional certification exams. You will take a computerized, proctored exam. You will have 4 hours to complete 125 questions. That means you will have, on average, roughly 2 minutes per question. The questions are all multiple choice. The exam can be taken through the ECC Exam Center or at a Pearson VUE center.

Should you want to take your certification even further, you could go after the CEH Practical exam. For this exam you must perform an actual penetration test and write a report at the end of it. This demonstrates that in addition to knowing the body of material covered by the exam, you can put that knowledge to use in a practical way. You will be expected to know how to compromise systems and identify vulnerabilities.

To pass the exam, you will have to correctly answer a certain number of questions, though the actual number will vary. The passing grade varies depending on the difficulty of the questions asked. The harder the questions that are asked out of the complete pool of questions, the fewer questions you need to get right to pass the exam. If you get easier questions, you will need to get more of the questions right to pass. There are some sources of information that will tell you that you need to get 70 percent of the questions right, and that may be okay for general guidance and preparation as a rough low-end marker. However, keep in mind that when you sit down to take the actual test at the testing center, the passing grade will vary. The score you will need to achieve will range from 60 to 85 percent.

The good news is that you will know whether you passed before you leave the testing center. You will get your score when you finish the exam, and you will also get a piece of paper indicating the details of your grade. You will get feedback associated with the different scoring areas and how you performed in each of them.

Who Is Eligible

Not everyone is eligible to sit for the CEH exam. Before you go too far down the road, you should check your qualifications. Just as a starting point, you have to be at least 18 years of age. The other eligibility standards are as follows:

- Anyone who has versions 1–7 of the CEH certification. The CEH certification is ANSI certified now, but early versions of the exam were available before the certification. Anyone who wants to take the ANSI-accredited certification who has the early version of the CEH certification can take the exam.

- Minimum of two years of related work experience. Anyone who has the experience will have to pay a nonrefundable application fee of $100.
- Have taken an EC-Council training.

If you meet these qualification standards, you can apply for the certification, along with paying the fee if it is applicable to you (if you take one of the EC-Council trainings, the fee is included). The application will be valid for three months.

Further Resources

Finally, this exam book should not be the only resource you use to prepare. You should use other exam books and study guides as well. The more diverse the exposure in terms of reading and preparation material, the better. Take your time studying; invest at least one hour per day prior to your exam date.

If you have not already read *CEHv11: Certified Ethical Hacker Version 11 Study Guide* (Sybex, 2021) and you're not seeing passing grades on these practice tests, it is an excellent resource to master any CEH topics causing problems. The study guide maps every official exam objective to the corresponding chapter in the book to help track your exam preparation objective by objective. There are also challenging review questions in each chapter to prepare for exam day and online test prep materials including flashcards and additional practice tests.

How to Register for the Online Testbanks

All the questions in this book are also available in Sybex's online practice test tool. To get access to this online learning environment, go to www.wiley.com/go/sybextestprep and start by registering your book. You'll receive a PIN code and instructions on where to create an online test bank account. Once you have access, you can use the online version to create your own sets of practice tests from the book questions and practice in a timed and graded setting.

Chapter

1

Practice Test 1

1.   Which of the following is considered a passive reconnaissance action?

   A.   Searching through the local paper

   B.   Calling Human Resources

   C.   Using the nmap -sT command

   D.   Conducting a man-in-the-middle attack

2.   Which encryption was selected by NIST as the principal method for providing confidentiality after the DES algorithm?

   A.   3DES

   B.   Twofish

   C.   RC4

   D.   AES

3.   What cloud service would you be most likely to use if you wanted to share documents with another person?

   A.   Software as a Service

   B.   Platform as a Service

   C.   Storage as a Service

   D.   Infrastructure as a Service

4.   What is the difference between a traditional firewall and an IPS?

   A.   Firewalls don't generate logs.

   B.   An IPS cannot drop packets.

   C.   An IPS does not follow rules.

   D.   An IPS can inspect and drop packets.

5.   What is one of the advantages of IPv6 over IPv4 from a security perspective?

   A.   IPv4 has a smaller address space.

   B.   IPv6 allows for header authentication.

   C.   IPv6 is more flexible about extensions.

   D.   IPv6 is typically represented in hexadecimal.

6.   You are the senior manager in the IT department for your company. What is the most cost-effective way to prevent social engineering attacks?

   A.   Install HIDS.

   B.   Ensure that all patches are up-to-date.

   C.   Monitor and control all email activity.

   D.   Implement security awareness training.

7.   In which phase within the ethical hacking framework do you alter or delete log information?

   A.   Scanning and enumeration

   B.   Gaining access

   C.   Reconnaissance

   D.   Covering tracks

8. An attacker is conducting the following on the target workstation: `nmap -sT 192.33.10.5`. The attacker is in which phase?

    A. Covering tracks

    B. Enumeration

    C. Scanning and enumeration

    D. Gaining access

9. Which encryption algorithm is a symmetric stream cipher?

    A. AES

    B. ECC

    C. RC4

    D. PGP

10. What is the most important part of conducting a penetration test?

    A. Receiving a formal written agreement

    B. Documenting all actions and activities

    C. Remediating serious threats immediately

    D. Maintaining proper handoff with the information assurance team

11. You are a CISO for a giant tech company. You are charged with implementing an encryption cipher for your new mobile devices that will be introduced in 2022. What encryption standard will you most likely choose?

    A. RC4

    B. MD5

    C. AES

    D. Skipjack

12. What does a SYN scan accomplish?

    A. It establishes a full TCP connection.

    B. It establishes only a "half open" connection.

    C. It opens an ACK connection with the target.

    D. It detects all closed ports on the target system.

13. What is the major vulnerability for an ARP request?

    A. It sends out an address request to all the hosts on the LAN.

    B. The address is returned with a username and password in cleartext.

    C. The address request can cause a DoS.

    D. The address request can be spoofed with the attacker's MAC address.

14. You are the CISO for a popular social website. Your engineers are telling you they are seeing multiple authentication failures but with multiple usernames, none of them ever repeated. What type of attack are you seeing?

    A. Brute force password attack

    B. Authentication failure attack

    C. Denial-of-service attack

    D. Credential stuffing attack

15. What is the purpose of a man-in-the-middle attack?

    A. Gaining access

    B. Maintaining access

    C. Hijacking a session

    D. Covering tracks

16. What method of exploitation might allow the adversary to pass arbitrary SQL queries within the URL?

    A. SQL injection

    B. XSS

    C. Spear phishing

    D. Ruby on Rails injection method

17. What is the default TTL value for Microsoft Windows 10 OS?

    A. 64

    B. 128

    C. 255

    D. 256

18. Which input value would you utilize in order to evaluate and test for SQL injection vulnerabilities?

    A. SQL test

    B. admin and password

    C. || or |!

    D. 1=1'

19. What is the advantage of using SSH for command-line traffic?

    A. SSH encrypts the traffic and credentials.

    B. You cannot see what the adversary is doing.

    C. Data is sent in the clear.

    D. A and B.

20. What year did the Ping of Death first appear?

    A. 1992

    B. 1989

    C. 1990

    D. 1996

21. Which type of malware is likely the most impactful?

    A. Worm

    B. Dropper

    C. Ransomware

    D. Virus

22. You are part of the help desk team. You receive a ticket from one of your users that their computer is periodically slow. The user also states that from time to time, documents have either disappeared or have been moved from their original location to another. You remote desktop to the user's computer and investigate. Where is the most likely place to see if any new processes have started?

    A. The Processes tab in Task Manager

    B. `C:\Temp`

    C. The Logs tab in Task Manager

    D. `C:\Windows\System32\User`

23. Your security team notifies you that they are seeing the same SSID being advertised in your vicinity, but the BSSID is different from ones they are aware of. What type of attack is this?

    A. Deauthentication attack

    B. Wardriving

    C. MAC spoofing

    D. Evil twin

24. What does a checksum indicate?

    A. That the data has made it to its destination

    B. That the three-way TCP/IP handshake finished

    C. That there were changes to the data during transit or at rest

    D. The size of the data after storage

25. Out of the following, which is one of RSA's registered key strengths?

    A. 1,024 bits

    B. 256 bits

    C. 128 bits

    D. 512 bits

26. To provide non-repudiation for email, which algorithm would you choose to implement?

  A. AES

  B. DSA

  C. 3DES

  D. Skipjack

27. Which of the following describes a race condition?

  A. Where two conditions occur at the same time and there is a chance that arbitrary commands can be executed with a user's elevated permissions, which can then be used by the adversary

  B. Where two conditions cancel one another out and arbitrary commands can be used based on the user privilege level

  C. Where two conditions are executed under the same user account

  D. Where two conditions are executed simultaneously with elevated user privileges

28. Your end clients report that they cannot reach any website on the external network. As the network administrator, you decide to conduct some fact finding. Upon your investigation, you determine that you are able to ping outside of the LAN to external websites using their IP address. Pinging websites with their domain name resolution does not work. What is most likely causing the issue?

  A. The firewall is blocking DNS resolution.

  B. The DNS server is not functioning correctly.

  C. The external websites are not responding.

  D. An HTTP GET request is being dropped at the firewall, preventing it from going out.

29. You are the security administration for your local city. You just installed a new IPS. Other than plugging it in and applying some basic IPS rules, no other configuration has been made. You come in the next morning, and you discover that there was so much activity generated by the IPS in the logs that it is too time-consuming to view. What most likely caused the huge influx of logs from the IPS?

  A. The clipping level was established.

  B. A developer had local admin rights.

  C. The LAN experienced a switching loop.

  D. The new rules were poorly designed.

30. Which method would be targeting the client in a web-based communication?

  A. Cross-site scripting (XSS)

  B. SQL injection

  C. XML external entity

  D. Command injection

31. As a penetration tester, only you and a few key selected individuals from the company will know of the targeted network that will be tested. You also have zero knowledge of your target other than the name and location of the company. What type of assessment is this called?

    A. Gray box testing

    B. White box testing

    C. Black box testing

    D. Blue box testing

32. As an attacker, you are searching social media sites as well as job listings. What phase of the attack are you in?

    A. Casing the target

    B. Gaining access

    C. Maintaining access

    D. Reconnaissance

33. Which scanning tool is more likely going to yield accurate and useful results during reconnaissance and enumeration?

    A. ncat

    B. Nmap

    C. ping

    D. nslookup

34. Why would an attacker conduct an open TCP connection scan using Nmap?

    A. The attacker does not want to attack the system.

    B. The attacker made a mistake by not selecting a SYN scan function.

    C. The attacker is trying to connect to network services.

    D. The attacker is trying to make the scan look like normal traffic.

35. Why would an attacker want to avoid tapping into a fiber-optic line?

    A. It costs a lot of money to tap into a fiber line.

    B. If done wrong, it could cause the entire connection signal to drop, therefore bringing unwanted attention from the targeted organization.

    C. The network traffic would slow down significantly.

    D. Tapping the line could alert an IPS/IDS.

36. You are an attacker who has successfully infiltrated your target's web server. You performed a web defacement on the targeted organization's website, and you were able to create your own credential with administrative privileges. Before conducting data exfiltration, what is the next move?

    A. Log into the new user account that you created.

    B. Go back and delete or edit the logs.

    C. Ensure that you log out of the session.

    D. Ensure that you migrate to a different session and log out.

37. What is a common attack type of the Kerberos protocol that can look like legitimate traffic?

　　A. Kerberoasting

　　B. Javaroasting

　　C. Man-in-the-middle

　　D. Ticket granting compromise

38. Where is the password file located on a Windows system?

　　A. `C:\Windows\temp`

　　B. `C:\Win\system\config`

　　C. `C:\Windows\accounts\config`

　　D. `C:\Windows\system32\config`

39. Which response would the adversary receive on closed ports if they conducted an XMAS scan?

　　A. RST

　　B. RST/ACK

　　C. No Response

　　D. FIN/ACK

40. Why would the adversary encode their payload before sending it to the target victim?

　　A. Encoding the payload will not provide any additional benefit.

　　B. By encoding the payload, the adversary actually encrypts the payload.

　　C. The encoded payload can bypass the firewall because there is no port associated with the payload.

　　D. Encoding the payload may bypass IPS/IDS detection because it changes the signature.

41. Which password is more secure?

　　A. keepyourpasswordsecuretoyourself

　　B. pass123!!

　　C. P@$$w0rD

　　D. KeepY0urPasswordSafe!

42. Which of the following best describes DNS poisoning?

　　A. The adversary intercepts and replaces the victim's MAC address with their own.

　　B. The adversary replaces their malicious IP address with the victim's IP address for the domain name.

　　C. The adversary replaces the legitimate domain name with the malicious domain name.

　　D. The adversary replaces the legitimate IP address that is mapped to the fully qualified domain name with the malicious IP address.

43. Which of the following allows the adversary to forge certificates for authentication?

   A. Wireshark

   B. Ettercap

   C. Cain & Abel

   D. Ncat

44. Which encryption standard is used in WEP?

   A. AES

   B. RC5

   C. MD5

   D. RC4

45. You are sitting inside of your office, and you notice a strange person in the parking lot with what appears to be a tall antenna connected to a laptop. What is the stranger most likely doing?

   A. Brute-forcing their personal electronic device

   B. Wardriving

   C. Warflying

   D. Bluesnarfing

46. If a web application is using a RESTful API, NoSQL databases, and microservices in containers, what style of design is it likely using?

   A. Model-view-controller

   B. Cloud-native design

   C. Traditional architecture

   D. NoSQL design

47. Which is the best example of a denial-of-service (DoS) attack?

   A. A victim's computer is infected with a virus.

   B. A misconfigured switch is in a switching loop.

   C. An adversary is forging a certificate.

   D. An adversary is consuming all available memory of a target system by opening as many "half-open" connections on a web server as possible.

48. In the Windows SAM file, what security identifier would indicate to the adversary that a given account is an administrator account?

   A. 500

   B. 1001

   C. ADM

   D. ADMIN_500

49. Which regional Internet registry is responsible for North and South America?

    A. RIPE

    B. AMERNIC

    C. LACNIC

    D. ARIN

50. Which of following actions is the last step in scanning a target?

    A. Scan for vulnerabilities

    B. Identify live systems

    C. Discover open ports

    D. Identify the OS and servers

51. Which of the following best describes the ICMP Type 8 code?

    A. Device is being filtered

    B. Network route is incorrect or missing

    C. Echo request

    D. Destination unreachable

52. Which of the following port ranges will show you the ports requiring administrative access?

    A. 0 to 1023

    B. 0 to 255

    C. 1024 to 49151

    D. 1 to 128

53. What is the length of an IPv6 address?

    A. 64 bits

    B. 128 bits

    C. 256 bits

    D. 32 bits

54. Which of the following switches for the Nmap command does nothing but fingerprinting an operating system?

    A. -O

    B. -sFRU

    C. -sA

    D. -sX

55. What command would the adversary use to show all the systems within the domain using the command-line interface in Windows?

   A. `netstat -R /domain`

   B. `net view /<domain_name>:domain`

   C. `net view /domain:<domain_name>`

   D. `netstat /domain:<domain_name>`

56. You are a passenger in an airport terminal. You glance across the terminal and notice a man peering over the shoulder of a young woman as she uses her tablet. What do you think he is doing?

   A. Wardriving

   B. Shoulder surfing

   C. War shouldering

   D. Shoulder jacking

57. What type of attack is being used if you were to see `<!ENTITY xxe SYSTEM "file:///etc/passwd">` in your web server logs?

   A. SQL injection

   B. XSS

   C. Command injection

   D. XXE

58. Which option describes the concept of injecting code into a portion of data in memory that allows for arbitrary commands to be executed?

   A. Buffer overflow

   B. Crash

   C. Heap spraying

   D. Format string

59. Of the following methods, which one acts as a middleman between an external network and the private network by initiating and establishing the connection?

   A. Proxy server

   B. Firewall

   C. Router

   D. Switch

60. As an attacker, you successfully exploited your target using a service that should have been disabled. The service had vulnerabilities that you were able to exploit with ease. There appeared to be a large cache of readily accessible information. What may be the issue here?

   A. The administrator did not apply the correct patches.

   B. The web server was improperly configured.

   C. You are dealing with a honeypot.

   D. The firewall was not configured correctly.

61. Where is the logfile that is associated with the activities of the last user that signed in within a Linux system?

    A. `/var/log/user_log`

    B. `/var/log/messages`

    C. `/var/log/lastlog`

    D. `/var/log/last_user`

62. What default TCP port does SSH utilize?

    A. Port 22

    B. Port 21

    C. Port 443

    D. Port 25

63. As a pen tester, you are hired to conduct an assessment on a group of systems for your client. You are provided with a list of critical assets, a list of domain controllers, and a list of virtual share drives. Nothing else was provided. What type of test are you conducting?

    A. White hat testing

    B. Gray hat testing

    C. Gray box testing

    D. Red hat testing

64. Which type of firewall would you use if you wanted to have the firewall check for malware as it passed through the firewall?

    A. Web application firewall

    B. Stateful firewall

    C. Next-generation firewall

    D. Stateless firewall

65. Which tool can be used to conduct layer 4 scanning and enumeration?

    A. Cain & Abel

    B. John the Ripper

    C. Ping-eater

    D. Nmap

66. What port number or numbers is/are associated with the IP protocol?

    A. 0 to 65535

    B. No ports

    C. 53

    D. 80

67. Which two protocols are connectionless?
    A. IP and TCP
    B. IP and FTP
    C. IP and UDP
    D. TCP and UDP

68. Into which phase of the MITRE ATT&CK framework does transmitting files found in an enterprise network by tunneling through DNS requests fall?
    A. Privilege escalation
    B. Persistence
    C. Exfiltration
    D. Defense evasion

69. What is patch management?
    A. Deploying patches when they are available
    B. Making determinations about patch disposition for business systems
    C. Deploying patches at the end of the month
    D. Determining what vulnerabilities are currently on your network and deploying patches immediately to eliminate the threat

70. At which layer of the OSI model does FTP reside?
    A. Session
    B. Application
    C. Network
    D. Transport

71. What open-source tool could you use to gather information about email addresses from various search providers?
    A. Nmap
    B. theHarvester
    C. Netcat
    D. John the Ripper

72. Which switch in Nmap invokes the XMAS scan?
    A. -sX
    B. -sS
    C. -xS
    D. -sT

73. Which of the following best describes fingerprinting?

    A. Scanning for vulnerabilities

    B. Using the -sX switch for Nmap

    C. Matching OS characteristics from a scan to a database in Nmap

    D. Checking to see what ports are open by firewalking

74. Which option describes a server-side attack targeting web applications?

    A. SQL injection

    B. Cross-site malware injection

    C. Cross-site scripting

    D. SQL site scripting

75. What port is used by DNS?

    A. 80

    B. 8080

    C. 53

    D. 25

76. In Linux, what file allows you to see user information such as full name, phone number, and office information?

    A. Shadow file

    B. Passwd file

    C. Userinfo file

    D. Useraccount file

77. What tool could you use to check flag settings in a TCP segment?

    A. Nmap

    B. SuperPing

    C. Ettercap

    D. Wireshark

78. Which type of packet does a Fraggle attack use to create a DoS attack?

    A. TCP

    B. IP

    C. ICMP

    D. UDP

79. Which instruction value is used to invoke a NOP (non-operating procedure)?

    A. 0x99

    B. 0x91

    C. 0xGH

    D. 0x90

80. What tool would you use to conduct banner grabbing?

A. aescrypt

B. Ettercap

C. netstat

D. Telnet

81. Which of the following functions is no longer utilized within IPv6?

A. Multicast

B. Anycast

C. Unicast

D. Broadcast

82. What are you creating when you set up a server with certain configurations and document step-by-step instructions?

A. Baseline

B. Procedure

C. Technical advisory

D. Guideline

83. Which application uses two ports?

A. Telnet

B. ICMP

C. HTTPS

D. FTP

84. Which of the following capabilities does the MegaPing tool not support?

A. Vulnerability detection

B. Scanning

C. Vulnerability exploitation

D. DNS name lookup

85. Which of the following is part of the account management lifecycle?

A. Account provisioning

B. Access denied

C. User authentication

D. None of the above

86. Which of the following activities describes the act of a person rummaging through a trash container looking for sensitive information?

    A. Trash jumping

    B. Dumpster party

    C. Trash diving

    D. Dumpster diving

87. What are two common ports used to connect to a web server?

    A. 80 and 25

    B. 80 and 8080

    C. 443 and 53

    D. 20 and 21

88. When considering the risks of local storage vs. third-party cloud storage, which statement is most accurate?

    A. Cloud storage is more secure because the commercial vendor has trained security professionals.

    B. When storage is local, you are responsible and accountable for the storage services.

    C. You can sue the cloud provider for damages.

    D. The cloud has more layers of security than traditional local storage infrastructures.

89. Which packet sniffing tool allows you to specify the individual fields you want printed in the output?

    A. Nmap

    B. tshark

    C. tcpdump

    D. Snoop

90. A classification label is associated with which of the following?

    A. A subject

    B. A file

    C. An object

    D. A folder

91. Which of the following tools allows you to create certificates that are not officially signed by a CA?

    A. Cain & Abel

    B. Nmap

    C. Ettercap

    D. Darkether

92. What type of social engineering attack uses SMS (text) messages to communicate with the victim?

    A. Smishing

    B. Vishing

    C. Phishing

    D. Kishing

93. This protocol is used for authentication purposes; it sends cleartext usernames and passwords with no forms of encryption or a means of challenging. What authentication protocol is this?

    A. CHAP

    B. POP

    C. PAP

    D. MSCHAP

94. What would you use "something you are" for?

    A. Challenge-response authentication

    B. Token-based authentication

    C. Single-factor authentication

    D. Multifactor authentication

95. When two or more authentication methods are used, what is it called?

    A. Multitiered authentication factor

    B. Multifactor authentication

    C. Multicommon factor authentication

    D. Multiauthentication factor

96. Which of the following has no key associated with it?

    A. MD5

    B. AES

    C. Skipjack

    D. PGP

97. What type of authentication is used in WPA2 to ensure the validity of both the client and the access point?

    A. Two-way handshake

    B. Three-way handshake

    C. Four-way handshake

    D. Five-way handshake

98. Which operating system build provides a suite of tools for network offensive (attack your target) purposes?

    A. Kali Linux

    B. Windows Server 2012 R2

    C. FreeBSD

    D. Security Onion

99. What is a major drawback of most antivirus software?

    A. It can be extremely slow.

    B. It must have the latest virus definitions.

    C. It can take up a lot of host resources.

    D. It requires a lot of effort to administer.

100. What is the value of using the four-way handshake in WPA2?

    A. Encrypts traffic

    B. Prevents replay attacks

    C. Ensures multifactor authentication is in use

    D. Performs host checking

101. What is the maximum byte size for a UDP datagram payload?

    A. 65,535

    B. 65,507

    C. 1,500

    D. 65,527

102. As an attacker, which of the following resources would be the best place to begin reconnaissance of your target?

    A. Nmap using the −s0 switch

    B. Suricata

    C. LinkedIn

    D. Calling the help desk masquerading as an authorized user

103. When sending a packet with a FIN flag set, what will the target respond with if the port is open?

    A. RST is returned.

    B. No response is returned.

    C. RST/ACK is returned.

    D. SYN/ACK is returned.

104. What is the result of conducting a MAC flood on a switch?

    A. The switch would fail to respond.

    B. It would create a DoS.

    C. The switch would operate as if it were a hub.

    D. The switch would continue to operate as normal.

105. Which of the following is the correct way to search for a specific IP address in Wireshark using a display filter?

    A. `ip.addr = 192.168.1.100`

    B. `ip == 192.168.1.100`

    C. `ip = 192.168.1.199`

    D. `ip.addr == 192.168.1.100`

106. Which of the following denial-of-service attacks would be most likely to be successful today?

    A. Fraggle

    B. Smurf

    C. Slowloris

    D. None of the above

107. An email contains a link with the subject line "Congratulations on your cruise!" and is sent to the finance person at a company. The email instructs the reader to click a hyperlink to claim the cruise. When the link is clicked, the reader is presented with a series of questions within an online form, such as name, Social Security number, and date of birth. What type of attack would this be considered?

    A. Email phishing

    B. Spear phishing

    C. Social engineering

    D. Identity theft

108. What is a network of zombie computers used to execute a DDoS on a target system called?

    A. Botnet

    B. Whaling

    C. Social engineering

    D. DoS

109. Cipher locks, mantraps, and bollards are considered what?

    A. Physical controls

    B. Technical controls

    C. Crime prevention through environmental design

    D. Physical barriers

110. Which of the following describes the X.509 standard?

    A. It defines the LDAP structure.

    B. It is a symmetric encryption algorithm.

    C. It uses a sandbox method for security.

    D. It describes the standard for creating a digital certificate.

111. Which of the following best describes steganography?

    A. A symmetric encryption algorithm

    B. Allowing the public to use your private key

    C. Hiding information within a picture or concealing it in an audio format

    D. Encrypting data using transposition and substitution

112. What process would you use to help ensure only the right people got access to sensitive information?

    A. Data classification

    B. Data masking

    C. Data encryption

    D. Data processing

113. What do we call the model used to determine who has to handle patching of systems at a cloud services provider?

    A. Shared responsibility

    B. Bell-LaPadula

    C. Carnegie Mellon Maturity

    D. Ford model

114. What is the governing council of the CEH exam?

    A. $(ISC)^2$

    B. EC-Council

    C. CompTIA

    D. Microsoft

115. What Transport layer protocol does DHCP operate with?

    A. IP

    B. TCP

    C. ICMP

    D. UDP

116. According the following screen shot, what is the IANA ID?

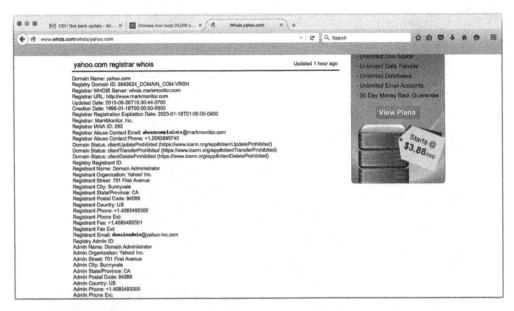

- **A.** 292
- **B.** 94089
- **C.** US
- **D.** 4083493300

117. According to the following screen shot, what process identification is Terminal running?

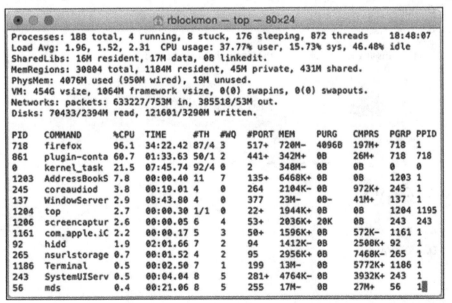

    A. 1

    B. 708

    C. 243

    D. 1186

118. As shown in the following image, what type of attack is being conducted?

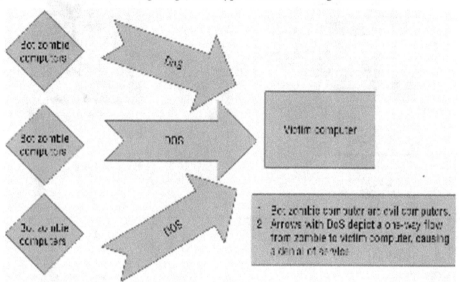

    A. Fraggle

    B. DDoS

    C. DoS

    D. Bot attack

119. What is missing to complete the three-way handshake shown here?

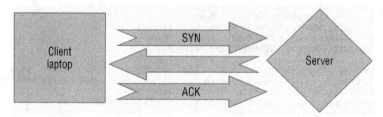

    A. ACK/SYN

    B. ACK

    C. TCP/IP

    D. SYN/ACK

120. In the following screen shot, which process is taking 386 MB of memory from the computer?

```
● ● ●                    rblockmon — top — 80×24
Processes: 178 total, 2 running, 5 stuck, 171 sleeping, 690 threads    19:56:57
Load Avg: 1.80, 1.71, 2.06  CPU usage: 2.69% user, 2.69% sys, 94.60% idle
SharedLibs: 16M resident, 17M data, 0B linkedit.
MemRegions: 38420 total, 935M resident, 39M private, 394M shared.
PhysMem: 3999M used (979M wired), 94M unused.
VM: 429G vsize, 1064M framework vsize, 0(0) swapins, 256(0) swapouts.
Networks: packets: 825122/933M in, 544300/107M out.
Disks: 88320/2643M read, 161873/4126M written.

PID   COMMAND      %CPU TIME      #TH  #WQ  #PORT MEM    PURG   CMPRS  PGRP PPID
718   firefox      4.0  46:24.62  65   0    506   608M   0B     288M   718  1
0     kernel_task  2.9  10:15.34  92/4 0    2     386M   0B     0B     0    0
861   plugin-conta 5.3  08:23.21  21   0    326   110M+  0B     74M    718  718
875   soffice      0.0  03:40.23  9    1    253   93M    0B     35M    875  1
137   WindowServer 1.9  09:43.67  4    0    377   36M    44K    46M    137  1
244   Finder       0.0  00:07.46  3    0    256   21M    44K    20M    244  1
1186  Terminal     0.6  00:04.84  7    1    210   11M    0B     8004K  1186 1
215   mds_stores   0.0  00:34.61  3    1    54    11M    520K   15M    215  1
759   VTDecoderXPC 0.0  00:41.84  8    0    72    11M    0B     6660K  759  1
268   CalendarAgen 0.0  00:10.77  4    0    172   10M    0B     14M    268  1
56    mds          0.0  00:27.93  3    0    242   7964K  0B     32M    56   1
1     launchd      0.0  00:13.10  5    4    3160  7648K  0B     5700K  1    0
88    loginwindow  0.0  00:05.17  2    0    368   6640K  8192B  10M    88   1
285   Notification 0.0  00:02.23  3    0    198   6612K  0B     7340K  285  1
```

A. Firefox

B. kernel_task

C. Finder

D. WindowServer

121. What type of attack is shown in the following image?

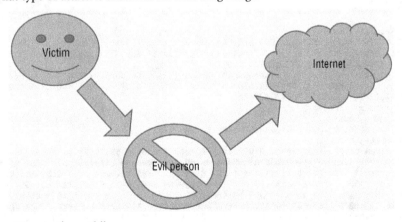

A. Man-in-the-middle

B. DoS

C. DDoS

D. Spear phishing

122. Under which scan has the most ports been scanned?

- **A.** Ping
- **B.** SYN stealth
- **C.** SYN
- **D.** DUP

123. As shown in the following screen shot, what type of algorithm was used to hash the user password?

A. SHA-512

B. Kerberos

C. AES

D. SHA-256

124. Which file or application has the permission set with 644?

```
● ● ●                   💾 Macintosh HD — bash — 80×24
Rays-MBP:/ rblockmon$ ls -l
total 45
drwxrwxr-x+ 47 root   admin   1598 Nov 14 13:50 Applications
drwxr-xr-x+ 60 root   wheel   2040 Nov 11 18:20 Library
drwxr-xr-x@  2 root   wheel     68 Sep  9  2014 Network
drwxr-xr-x+  4 root   wheel    136 Oct 29  2014 System
drwxr-xr-x   6 root   admin    204 Oct 29  2014 Users
drwxrwxrwt@  4 root   admin    136 Nov 20 20:41 Volumes
drwxr-xr-x@ 39 root   wheel   1326 Sep  2 16:02 bin
drwxrwxr-t@  2 root   admin     68 Sep  9  2014 cores
dr-xr-xr-x   3 root   wheel   4322 Nov 20 16:53 dev
lrwxr-xr-x@  1 root   wheel     11 Oct 29  2014 etc -> private/etc
dr-xr-xr-x   2 root   wheel      1 Nov 21 20:55 home
-rw-r--r--@  1 root   wheel    313 Oct  1  2014 installer.failurerequests
dr-xr-xr-x   2 root   wheel      1 Nov 21 20:55 net
drwxr-xr-x@  6 root   wheel    204 Oct 29  2014 private
drwxr-xr-x@ 59 root   wheel   2006 Sep  2 16:02 sbin
lrwxr-xr-x@  1 root   wheel     11 Oct 29  2014 tmp -> private/tmp
drwxr-xr-x@ 10 root   wheel    340 Oct 29  2014 usr
lrwxr-xr-x@  1 root   wheel     11 Oct 29  2014 var -> private/var
Rays-MBP:/ rblockmon$ ▉
```

A. usr

B. net

C. Volumes

D. installer.failurerequests

125. From the information given in the Wireshark pcap file, what operating system is the source connecting to a web server?

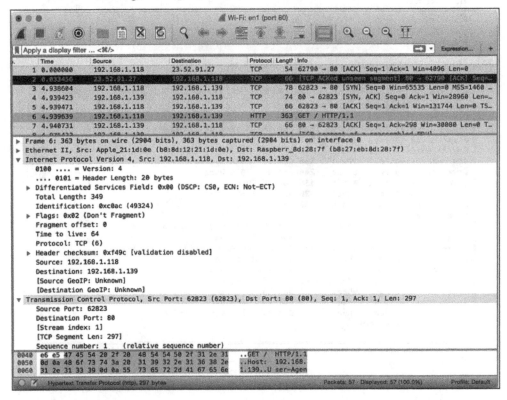

    A. OS X

    B. Microsoft

    C. Linux

    D. Raspbian

Chapter

2

Practice Test 2

1. Which of the following is considered an administrative control?
    A. Biometric device
    B. Mantrap
    C. Security policy
    D. Access control list

2. If a company has been given a /24 network from its Internet service provider, what CIDR notation would need to be used for each network if the company needed to have eight networks out of that allocation?
    A. /27
    B. /26
    C. /28
    D. /8

3. What is the default port number for Telnet?
    A. 21
    B. 23
    C. 53
    D. 443

4. What is the protocol commonly used for key exchange, where the keys are mutually derived rather than directly exchanged?
    A. OAKLEY
    B. AES
    C. Diffie-Hellman
    D. PGP

5. Which algorithm does not provide integrity or confidentiality?
    A. DSA
    B. AES
    C. RC4
    D. PGP

6. Which of the following acronyms represent the institution that governs North America IP space?
    A. ICANN
    B. PIR
    C. ARIN
    D. APNIC

7. At what layer of the OSI model does ARP reside?

   A. Presentation layer

   B. Application layer

   C. Physical layer

   D. Network layer

8. What technique would a malware author use to try to make it past an anti-malware solution?

   A. Disassembly

   B. Obfuscation

   C. Reverse engineering

   D. Dropper

9. What tool could you use locally on a Kali Linux or Parrot OS system to look for exploits available across different platforms, which may also provide exploit source code?

   A. Empire

   B. Metasploit

   C. Nmap

   D. searchsploit

10. Which Nmap parameter would allow you to perform tasks like getting the Server Message Block workgroup a system is in?

   A. `--script`

   B. `-sScript`

   C. `-sSMB`

   D. `-sX`

11. Which of these is a GUI tool that runs under Windows and can be used to perform ping sweeps and port scans?

   A. MegaPing

   B. Ettercap

   C. Dsniff

   D. Nmap

12. What key sizes in bits are used within AES?

   A. 64 and 128

   B. 128, 192, and 256

   C. 128 and 256

   D. 256

13. Which of these is an exploit that takes advantage of a vulnerability in the Server Message Block protocol to compromise systems remotely?

    A. WannaCry

    B. BigBlue

    C. EternalBlue

    D. ShadowBrokers

14. Which of the following protocols would be most likely to be used to manage a botnet?

    A. HTTP

    B. DNS

    C. SMTP

    D. ICMP

15. You are team leader for your financial firm. You set a policy in place that all coworkers must clean off their desk, empty trash, shred sensitive documents, and secure other critical documents in their respective containers at the end of the day. What is the common name for such a policy?

    A. Clean room policy

    B. Clean desk policy

    C. Sanitization policy

    D. Wrapping up policy

16. You work for an organization that has several buildings spread over an area about two square miles. What would you call the network your organization is using if all the buildings were connected together?

    A. Wide area network

    B. Mesh area network

    C. Local area network

    D. Metropolitan area network

17. What type of firewall would operate at layer 7 of the OSI model?

    A. Stateful firewall

    B. Deep packet inspection firewall

    C. Web application firewall

    D. Access control list

18. If you were developing a RESTful API, implemented at a cloud services provider, what application model would you most likely be using within the cloud services space?

    A. Monolithic

    B. N-tier

    C. Microservices

    D. Model-view-controller

19. What is another term for *masquerading?*

  A. Doppelganger

  B. Ghost

  C. Impersonation

  D. Dual persona

20. Malware installed at the kernel is very difficult to detect with products such as antivirus and anti-malware programs. What is this type of malware called?

  A. Ransomware

  B. Rootkit

  C. Vampire tap

  D. Worm

21. What are the security functions described by the NIST Cybersecurity Framework?

  A. Protect, Detect, Respond

  B. Plan, Do, Check, Act

  C. Identify, Plan, Check, Recover

  D. Identify, Protect, Detect, Respond, Recover

22. Which of the following password cracking methods is the fastest?

  A. Dictionary attack

  B. Brute force

  C. Birthday attack

  D. Reverse hash matching

23. In Linux, what designator is used to uniquely identify a user account?

  A. GID

  B. SID

  C. UID

  D. PID

24. Using Nmap, which switch command enables a UDP connections scan of a host?

  A. -sS

  B. -sX

  C. -PT

  D. -sU

25. Which of the following best indicates a top-level parent domain?

  A. sybex.com

  B. .org

  C. www.wiley.com

  D. www.

26. Based on the following tcpdump output, what is the port number the client is sending to?

```
    192.168.4.111.64165 > 17.248.189.5.https: Flags [P.], cksum
0x3fc3 (correct), seq 1367415277:1367416602, ack 528485940, win
2048, options [nop,nop,TS val 1065783570 ecr 3032585554], length
1325
```

A. 80

B. 23

C. 443

D. 8080

27. You are a security administrator working at a movie production company. One of your daily duties is to check the IDS logs when you are alerted. You notice that you received a lot of incomplete three-way handshakes, your memory performance has been dropping significantly on your web server, and customers are complaining of really slow connections. What could be the actual issue?

A. DoS

B. DDoS

C. Smurf attack

D. SYN flood

28. If you needed to capture traffic going to and coming from an individual user's workstation and you had access to a Cisco switch where the user was connected, what type of port should you configure and use to capture traffic?

A. SPAN

B. SPAM

C. Trunk

D. STP

29. If you wanted to redirect traffic to a particular hostname on the Internet to a server that you had control of, what type of attack could you use?

A. ARP spoofing

B. DNS spoofing

C. Masquerading

D. Man-in-the-middle

30. You've just compromised a system using Metasploit. What module would you now load to collect passwords from memory?

A. dumphash

B. autoroute

C. mimikatz

D. siddump

31. Which of the following provides free information about a website that includes phone numbers, administrator's email, and even the domain registration authority?

   A. nslookup

   B. dig

   C. Whois.net

   D. Ping

32. What is significant about RFC 1918?

   A. It signifies non-routable IP addresses.

   B. It signifies the use of web proxy servers.

   C. It describes the usage of DMZs.

   D. It covers the authentication header in IPSec.

33. What utility could you use if you wanted to be specific about individual fields to set while you were sending network messages to gather information about remote hosts?

   A. hping

   B. Ettercap

   C. Nmap

   D. pingcraft

34. A traditional HIDS uses which method for detection?

   A. Signature base

   B. Anomaly base

   C. Firewall rules

   D. Statistically anomaly

35. Which of the following verifies a user's authenticity when the user is requesting a certificate?

   A. Certificate authority

   B. Certificate revocation list

   C. X.509 and Kerberos

   D. Organizational unit (OU)

36. An attacker is using different methods of cracking an encryption algorithm, such as side channel attacks, frequency analysis, and also bit flipping. What is the attacker doing?

   A. Brute-forcing

   B. Cracking credentials

   C. Digital forensics

   D. Cryptanalysis

37. What are the two types of wireless network?

  A. Passive, active

  B. Point-to-point, multicast

  C. Infrastructure, active

  D. Ad hoc, infrastructure

38. To sniff, what mode must your network adapter be configured to in order to pull frames off an Ethernet or wireless network that aren't addressed to you?

  A. Active

  B. Promiscuous

  C. Stealth

  D. CSMA/CD mode

39. Which authentication protocol is used in WPA2?

  A. CCMP

  B. 3DES

  C. AES

  D. LEAP

40. You are an administrator overseeing IT security operations for a local bank. As you review logs from the prior day, you notice a very high rate of UDP packets targeting your web server that are coming from your clients all at the same time. What could be the culprit?

  A. Smurf attack

  B. DDoS

  C. SYN flood attack

  D. Fraggle attack

41. Which is the last step in the TCP three-way handshake?

  A. ACK

  B. SYN

  C. SYN/ACK

  D. FIN

42. If your organization is using Google's GSuite for email and document editing, what type of cloud service are you making use of?

  A. Software as a Service

  B. Storage as a Service

  C. Infrastructure as a Service

  D. Platform as a Service

43. As part of an assessment on an organization you working for, you decide to conduct a social engineering attack to gather credentials that you will use later. What type of attack would be the most efficient if you wanted to get credentials from an administrator?

   A. Man-in-the-middle

   B. Pharming

   C. Spear phishing

   D. Phishing

44. What would you expect a general-purpose computer to have that an IoT device wouldn't have?

   A. Keyboard

   B. Memory

   C. Processor

   D. Storage

45. Which of the following describes a "soft" control?

   A. User agreement

   B. Access control list

   C. Biometrics

   D. Security clerk

46. What capability does a backdoor provide to the adversary?

   A. Backdoors can corrupt data software.

   B. They destroy cryptographic keys in the TPM.

   C. They provide low-level formatting operations.

   D. They provide remote access to the client.

47. Which of the following describes the collection of human physical attributes for use in performing electronic authentication?

   A. Personal identification card

   B. Hair and fingerprints

   C. Biometrics

   D. Type 3 control

48. Which of these is not used for biometrics?

   A. Voice

   B. Iris

   C. Hair

   D. Fingerprint

49. Which of the following compares two hash values in order to provide non-repudiation?

    A. DSA

    B. ECE

    C. MD5

    D. SHA-1

50. During the course of testing, you identify a WAP that you are going to exploit. You discover that the WAP is using WEP. Which method will you utilize in order to exploit the WAP?

    A. The encryption algorithm, which is RC4

    B. The initialization vector (IV)

    C. The password

    D. The username and password

51. You have just completed the footprinting phase of your attack and are ready to move on by operating an assortment of tools to gather intelligence on your target. You were able to determine what services are being offered on ports. You were able to see what accounts are available and to identify different sharing services as well. What phase were you operating within?

    A. Service proxy

    B. Impassive scanning

    C. Fingerprinting

    D. Enumeration

52. Using Nmap, what is the correct command to scan a target subnet of 192.168.0.0/24 using a ping sweep and identifying operating systems?

    A. `nmap -sn -O 192.168.0.0/24`

    B. `nmap -sN -V 192.168.0.0/24`

    C. `nmap -sT -P 192.168.0.0/24`

    D. `nmap -Ps -O 192.168.0.0/24`

53. Which of the following services is registered for port 110?

    A. SNMP

    B. RPC

    C. POP3

    D. LDAP

54. If you needed to perform a lookup of a hostname from an IP address, what utility could you use?

    A. Ping

    B. Nmap

    C. Hostcheck

    D. dig

55. What common technique is used to extend a company's network to employee systems when they are working from home?

   A. Segmentation

   B. VPN

   C. VLAN

   D. Isolation

56. Which of the following can you use to conduct banner grabbing?

   A. Telnet

   B. Ping

   C. `nmap -sP`

   D. `del *.*`

57. As a pen tester, what content might you include in addition to your general findings?

   A. List of patched systems

   B. List of disabled accounts

   C. List of identified vulnerabilities

   D. List of revoked certificates

58. What is the IEEE standard for port-based authentication?

   A. TACACS

   B. Diameter

   C. 802.1X

   D. TACACS+

59. Which of the following attacks sends fragmented UDP packets to a Windows system using port 53 or other UDP ports that may cause the system to crash?

   A. Fraggle

   B. Bonk

   C. Smash the stack

   D. Smurf

60. Which of the following is an application that does not need a host or human interaction to disrupt and corrupt data?

   A. Worm

   B. Virus

   C. Trojan

   D. Malware

61. Which application exploit type works against dynamic memory allocations?

A. Return to libc

B. Heap spraying

C. Buffer overflow

D. Stack smashing

62. Which of the following is a good practice that includes the ability to isolate systems and detect attacks and may also include preventive measures?

A. Defense in depth

B. Security measure

C. Baseline configuration

D. Defensible network architecture

63. What is one disadvantage of a single sign-on (SSO) strategy?

A. It offers a single point of failure for authentication.

B. There is no replication for security policies.

C. Passwords are stored in plain text.

D. User accounts are easily accessible.

64. What common protocol may be used to communicate with IoT devices on home or business networks?

A. SNMP

B. ICMP

C. SMTP

D. HTTP

65. Which of the following is an optimal way of discovering passwords in plain text?

A. Intercepting an SSH connection

B. Following a TCP stream

C. Intercepting SSL traffic

D. Cracking an account using John the Ripper

66. What is a content-addressable memory table?

A. A table of IP addresses

B. A table used to view NetBIOS names

C. A table of MAC addresses associated with ports

D. A list of domain names tied to IP addresses

67. What is the most important task you should perform as part of a penetration test?

A. Get informed approval

B. Write a report

C. Get a contract in place

D. Compromise all systems

68. Which of the following is the protocol used by Microsoft Windows systems for authentication from one system to another?

   A. SESAME

   B. Diameter

   C. Kerberos

   D. HIDS

69. What is the process that changes a private IP address to a public address at the gateway?

   A. NAT

   B. PRAT

   C. GNAT

   D. NAT-T

70. What are the two types of intrusion detection systems?

   A. NIDS and SIDS

   B. HIDS and SIDS

   C. IDS and IPS

   D. HIDS and NIDS

71. What site would you use to gather financial information about a company, including 10-K reports?

   A. EDGAR

   B. HAL

   C. MOLES

   D. Google

72. Which federal law mandates securing medical records at rest and in transit?

   A. PCI

   B. HIPAA

   C. FISMA

   D. PATRIOT Act

73. What is one advantage an attacker has over a defender/victim?

   A. Time

   B. TOR network forums

   C. Money

   D. Metasploit

74. Which of the following is associated with security access in a wireless network?

A. WPA

B. 802.1X

C. Radius

D. TACACS+

75. Which of the following deletes the Clients table within an SQL database?

A. UPDATE TABLE Clients

B. SELECT * FROM Clients

C. INSERT TABLE Clients

D. DROP TABLE Clients

76. Which of the following tools is used exclusively to scan for vulnerabilities on a target system or a network?

A. Snort

B. Ncat

C. Nessus

D. Metasploit

77. What utility is used to gather information about NetBIOS configurations on Windows systems?

A. netstat

B. Nmap

C. nbtstat

D. Ping

78. Which of the following encryption methods was developed by Phil Zimmerman?

A. AES

B. PGP

C. DES

D. DEA

79. What is the address length used by IPv6?

A. 32 bits

B. 128 bytes

C. 32 bytes

D. 128 bits

80. Which of the following best describes a vulnerability?

A. A threat being potentially realized

B. A weakness in a system

    C. A threat actor

    D. An incident

81. A new user in a company is given a minimal set of privileges. As they are promoted and move to different positions, they continue to gain more privileges. What is this called?

    A. Privilege creep

    B. Position creep

    C. Access creep

    D. Privilege escalation

82. What would you call a device on a network?

    A. A node

    B. A computer

    C. A switch

    D. An access device

83. What protocol could you use to gather configuration information about a system over the network?

    A. SMTP

    B. SNMP

    C. HTTP

    D. FTP

84. What operating-system-agnostic feature of Metasploit would you use to perform tasks on a compromised system, including getting keystrokes?

    A. Meterpreter

    B. Metainterpreter

    C. Spelunker

    D. Mimikatz

85. What is the purpose of the Internet Key Exchange (IKE) protocol?

    A. To transfer user data

    B. To collect user profiles

    C. To distribute keys to the public

    D. To exchange secret keys

86. In regard to biometrics, when the false reject rate (FRR) and the false acceptance rate (FAR) are equal, what does this intersection mean?

    A. Crossover error rate

    B. False equal rate

    C. Sum

    D. Crossover equal rate

87. An application that is designed to look like a known legitimate application but is actually malicious in nature is considered what type of malware?

    A. Spyware

    B. Rootkit

    C. Adware

    D. Trojan

88. What standard port does SFTP use?

    A. 20

    B. 21

    C. 22

    D. 20 and 21

89. What is the biggest problem with using rainbow tables for password cracking?

    A. Disk space utilization

    B. Processor utilization

    C. Low success rate

    D. Not used for password cracking

90. You are a system administrator for a law firm. You are informed that a few users are indicating that they are receiving email messages from the help desk asking for their username and password to confirm ticket creation. They indicate they have not opened any tickets with the help desk. What is likely going on?

    A. Smishing

    B. Phishing

    C. Vishing

    D. Fishing

91. Which of the following services is associated with TCP port 389?

    A. LDAP

    B. IMAP

    C. SMB

    D. RPC

92. A system creates a certificate with the assigned public and private keys. This system also digitally signs it. What is this system's role?

    A. Registration authority

    B. Certificate authority

    C. Kerberos system

    D. Server/client environment

93. As a security administrator, you want to ensure every user only has the specific permissions and rights they need for the role they have. What principle are you following?

   A. Role-based access control

   B. Least privilege

   C. Reducing availability

   D. Setting up an encryption process

94. Microsoft Office and other office suite applications have a feature that should be turned off to prevent malware from executing or spreading. What feature should be disabled?

   A. Mail

   B. FTP client

   C. Auto-update feature

   D. Macro feature

95. What is the name of the entity that may be used to hold certificates and keys in case the primary keys or certificates are unavailable?

   A. Government safe

   B. Hot site

   C. Escrow

   D. Offsite backup

96. What standard TCP port does HTTPS use?

   A. 443

   B. 8080

   C. 80

   D. 22

97. When a user authenticates once to a resource and is then permitted to access additional applications without the need to reauthenticate, what form of authentication is being used?

   A. Once sign-on

   B. Nonce sign-on

   C. Kerberos

   D. Single sign-on

98. What does a router separate?

   A. Collision domains

   B. Broadcast domains

   C. Switching domains

   D. Routing loops

99. What is the ICMP message used to allow the traceroute program to indicate hops?

   A. Port unavailable

   B. Host unreachable

   C. Source quench

   D. Time exceeded in transit

100. What do you call the PDU for UDP?

   A. Packet

   B. Segment

   C. Datagram

   D. Frame

101. The password file of a Windows system is located in which of the following directories?

   A. `C:\System32\Windows\config`

   B. `\etc\win\config`

   C. `C:\System\Windows\config`

   D. `C:\Windows\System32\config`

102. What is the act of guessing every possible password combination of an account?

   A. Brute force

   B. Pass the hash

   C. Dictionary attack

   D. Social engineering

103. What command would you use to give read, write, and execute privileges for an object to the owner, group, and others in Linux?

   A. `chmod 666`

   B. `chmod 777`

   C. `chmod 7`

   D. `chmod 532`

104. Which security principle is violated if data is corrupted by bad memory as it's being stored on a hard disk?

   A. Availability

   B. Confidentiality

   C. Integrity

   D. Possession

105. Which of the following is considered a framework for penetration testing?

   A. Metasploit

   B. Cain & Abel

    C. Nessus

    D. Security Onion

106. In Windows, what command can you use to hide a file?

    A. `+h attrib <filename>`

    B. `h+ <filename>`

    C. `filename attrib +h`

    D. `attrib +h <filename>`

107. Which of the following is a correct MAC address?

    A. 00-12-3e-ff-d4-98

    B. 3i-45-fa-90-25-1b

    C. ff-ff-ff-ff-ff-ff-fg

    D. 65-23-ab-cb-a9

108. A stateful firewall device operates at what layer of the OSI model?

    A. Layer 2

    B. Layer 4

    C. Layer 7

    D. Layer 3

109. What is one concern for using a SYN scan, even if you are going low and slow?

    A. Half-open connections.

    B. It's inaccurate.

    C. You are performing a full connect.

    D. Firewalls block all SYN messages.

110. What is the biggest drawback from using anti-malware software?

    A. It takes up processing resources.

    B. It must have up-to-date virus definitions.

    C. Anti-malware software is expensive.

    D. It can be centrally or independently administered.

111. What is the name of the algorithm that was selected to be the Advanced Encryption Standard?

    A. Rijndael

    B. Lucifer

    C. Feistel

    D. Skipjack

112. What do you call the process used to convert machine-level opcodes back to mnemonics that can be more easily read by humans?

   A. Decompilation

   B. Disassembly

   C. Decryption

   D. Disambiguation

113. A user reports that they have downloaded a music file from the Internet. They inform you that when they opened the file, it seemed as though it installed an application, and then the user was prompted to send a payment of $500 to a PayPal account to get the key to decrypt their hard drive. The user no longer has access to their desktop. What could be the issue?

   A. The user is experiencing a hoax.

   B. The user downloaded and installed ransomware.

   C. The user installed malware.

   D. The user downloaded the wrong music file.

114. What do you need to provide to Wireshark to allow it to decrypt encrypted packets?

   A. License

   B. Password

   C. Keys

   D. Hash

115. What type of infrastructure does this describe?

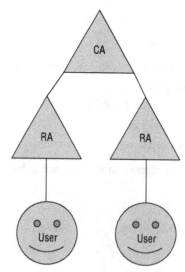

A. PKI

B. Man-in-the-middle attack

C. Social engineering

D. Kerberos environment

116. What type of protocol is primarily being used in this screen shot?

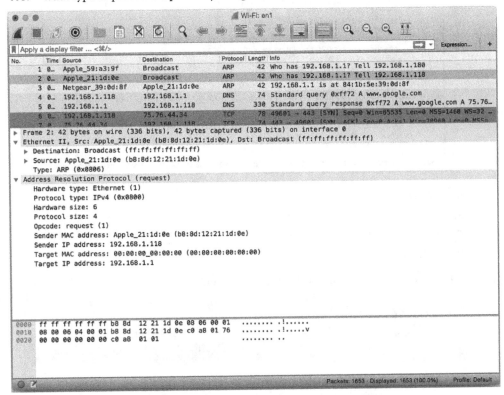

A. Broadcast

B. ARP request

C. Ping

D. DHCP lease

117. What IP address can you determine from the following diagram?

```
●●●                    🏠 rblockmon — bash — 80×24
Last login: Sun Nov 29 12:55:14 on ttys000
Rays-MBP:~ rblockmon$ ifconfig -a
lo0: flags=8049<UP,LOOPBACK,RUNNING,MULTICAST> mtu 16384
        options=3<RXCSUM,TXCSUM>
        inet6 ::1 prefixlen 128
        inet 127.0.0.1 netmask 0xff000000
        inet6 fe80::1%lo0 prefixlen 64 scopeid 0x1
        nd6 options=1<PERFORMNUD>
gif0: flags=8010<POINTOPOINT,MULTICAST> mtu 1280
stf0: flags=0<> mtu 1280
en0: flags=8863<UP,BROADCAST,SMART,RUNNING,SIMPLEX,MULTICAST> mtu 1500
        options=10b<RXCSUM,TXCSUM,VLAN_HWTAGGING,AV>
        ether 3c:07:54:31:ab:01
        nd6 options=1<PERFORMNUD>
        media: autoselect (none)
        status: inactive
en1: flags=8863<UP,BROADCAST,SMART,RUNNING,SIMPLEX,MULTICAST> mtu 1500
        ether b8:8d:12:21:1d:0e
        inet6 fe80::ba8d:12ff:fe21:1d0e%en1 prefixlen 64 scopeid 0x5
        inet 192.168.1.118 netmask 0xffffff00 broadcast 192.168.1.255
        nd6 options=1<PERFORMNUD>
        media: autoselect
        status: active
en2: flags=8963<UP,BROADCAST,SMART,RUNNING,PROMISC,SIMPLEX,MULTICAST> mtu 1500
```

- **A.** 192.168.1.255
- **B.** 192.168.1.118
- **C.** 255.255.255.255
- **D.** 192.168.1.1

118. What encoding type is being used in the screen shot?

    A. ASCII

    B. Hexadecimal

    C. Binary format

    D. UTF-8

119. What TLS version can be found in the following screen shot?

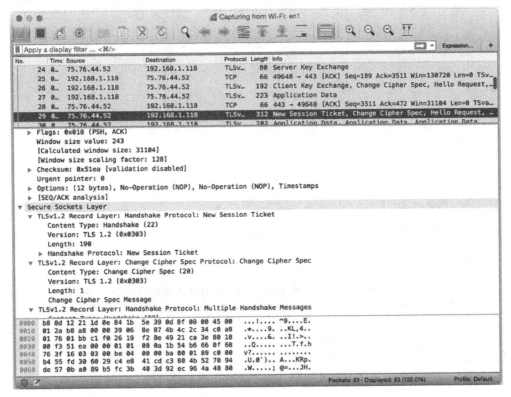

    A. 1.2

    B. 1.3

    C. 312

    D. 1

120. What is the adversary trying to do in the following screen shot?

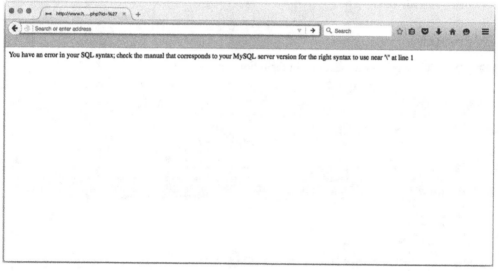

A. Ping of Death

B. Web server detection

C. SQL injection

D. Web defacement

121. As seen in the following screen shot, what is the adversary trying to do in the URL bar in the web browser?

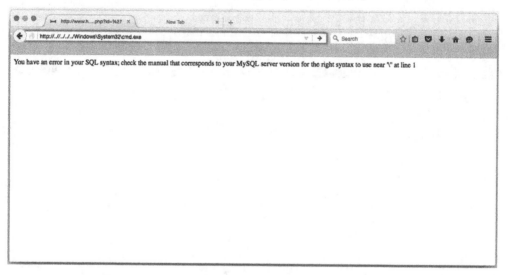

   A. Privilege escalation

   B. Directory traversal

   C. Blind SQL injection

   D. Deletion of a table in SQL

122. What DNS system is being queried by the client in the following screen shot?

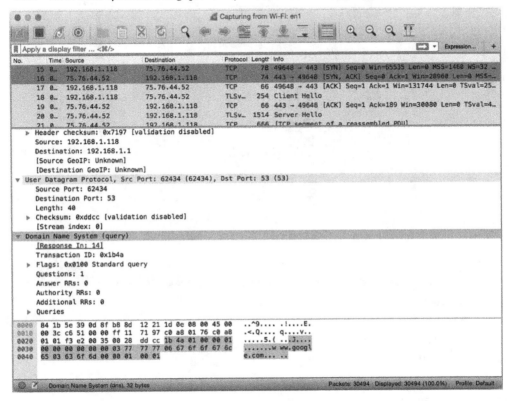

   A. Google

   B. Port 53

   C. Port 64234

   D. None

123. What is the password for the user root according to the following screen shot?

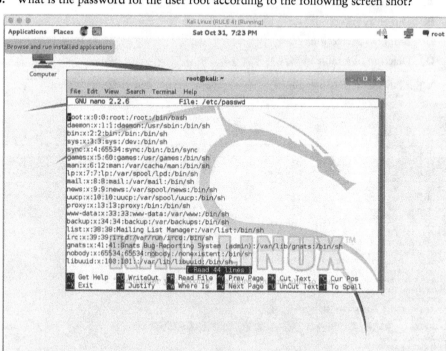

- **A.** root
- **B.** x
- **C.** There is no password.
- **D.** x:0:0

124. Based on the following log in Snort, what is the destination port to which the file is being downloaded?

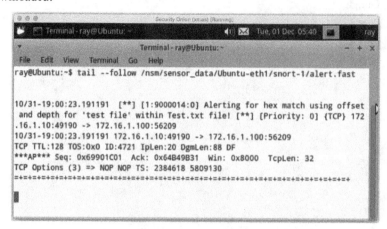

A. 56209

B. 23

C. 49190

D. The port is not available.

125. Which of the following is a user account?

```
colord:x:16733:0:99999:7:::
lightdm:x:16733:0:99999:7:::
avahi-autoipd:x:16733:0:99999:7:::
avahi:x:16733:0:99999:7:::
usbmux:x:16733:0:99999:7:::
kernoops:x:16733:0:99999:7:::
pulse:x:16733:0:99999:7:::
rtkit:x:16733:0:99999:7:::
speech-dispatcher:x:16733:0:99999:7:::
hplip:x:16733:0:99999:7:::
saned:x:16733:0:99999:7:::
mysql:x:16733:0:99999:7:::
ntp:x:16733:0:99999:7:::
sshd:x:16733:0:99999:7:::
sphinxsearch:x:16733:0:99999:7:::
prads:x:16733:0:99999:7:::
ossec:x:16733:0:99999:7:::
ossecm:x:16733:0:99999:7:::
ossecr:x:16733:0:99999:7:::
nobody:x:16733:0:99999:7:::
ray:$6$xHEKhMr2$95xeLgwRrKfDZ7QvhhGSt3bn2xFSqETvLgWJVJd7VcQiOj./eXJh4CG9fF1ls
yJu3E2Mvlno/iYxPocUNHrYd/:16733:0:99999:7:::
sguil:!:16739:0:99999:7:::
```

A. usbmux

B. ray

C. ossecr

D. nobody

Chapter

3

Practice Test 3

1. Which protocol is used for network management and can gather statistics and derive a current status from the node that it is operating on?

    A. NTP

    B. SMNP

    C. SSH

    D. SNMP

2. Which of the following is part of a DMZ but bridges access from organization to organization?

    A. Internet

    B. Extranet

    C. Intranet

    D. Outernet

3. How many subnets can be provided using a /26 Classless Inter-Domain Routing (CIDR) from a /24 allocation?

    A. 1

    B. 2

    C. 3

    D. 4

4. In a Linux system, where is the password file stored?

    A. /etc/passwd

    B. /etc/shadow

    C. /etc/user/password

    D. /shadow/etc

5. What command can you use to switch to a different user in Linux?

    A. swu

    B. user

    C. sudo

    D. su

6. What encryption algorithm is used within TLS for the handshake and key negotiation?

    A. AES

    B. RSA

    C. PGP

    D. ECE

7. Prior to deploying an anomaly-based detection system on a network, what must be achieved?

    A. Baseline

    B. Updated file definition

    C. Updated network infrastructure

    D. Patches pushed to clients before installation

8. Which of the following records determines a mail server in your domain?

    A. SOA

    B. CNAME

    C. A

    D. MX

9. What technique might you use if you had access to a local (physical) network but the network used switches and you wanted to see all the traffic?

    A. DNS poisoning

    B. Phishing

    C. ARP spoofing

    D. Packet fragmentation

10. What technique might you be able to use to get around older intrusion detection systems when sending traffic into a network?

    A. Fragmentation

    B. ARP spoofing

    C. DNS hijacking

    D. Phishing

11. You are a security administrator for an online dating website. Your logs are showing a lot of obfuscated PowerShell script execution. What do you think may be happening?

    A. Attacker is living off the land.

    B. Normal maintenance on servers.

    C. PowerShell is supposed to be encrypted.

    D. PowerShell is being updated.

12. The SAM log file entry is located in what part of a Windows Registry system?

    A. HKEY_LOCAL_MACHINE\SAM

    B. HKEY_LOCAL_SAM

    C. HKEY_LOCAL_MACHINE\WINDOWS

    D. HKEY_SYSTEM_MACHINE\SAME.L

13. Under which auxiliary in Metasploit can you scan for SNMP configurations?

    A. `auxiliary/snmp/scanner`

    B. `auxiliary/snmp/version`

    C. `auxiliary/scanner/snmp`

    D. `auxiliary/scan/snmp`

14. In Linux, what command is used to search for information inside files?

    A. `ser`

    B. `grep`

    C. `info >`

    D. `ls -l`

15. Which of the following tools is used to encode your payload in Metasploit?

    A. `msfconsole`

    B. `msfpayload`

    C. `encodesploit`

    D. `msfencode`

16. A system is compromised and is able to spawn a connection back to the adversary. What do you call the system or infrastructure the adversary is using to connect back to?

    A. Command and control

    B. Command processor

    C. Shellcode manager

    D. Command manager

17. What is a buffer used for?

    A. Dynamic data storage

    B. Static data storage

    C. Data in transit

    D. Processing power

18. What type of attack would the following code be vulnerable to?

```
char[5] attacker;
strcpy (attacker, "cat /etc/passwd");?
              scanf(&attacker);
```

    A. Buffer overflow

    B. SQL injection

    C. Command injection

    D. Heap spraying

19. What is the issue when there is no boundary being checked or validated in programming?

    A. The program will assign its own values.

    B. The program does not validate if the input values can be stored without overwriting the next memory segment.

    C. The program executes without checking what other programs are open.

    D. Memory allocation has already been reserved for a program.

20. When writing a program, what is one of the fundamental tasks that should be done when declaring a variable?

    A. Assign a random value to it.

    B. Do not assign a value because it can corrupt data.

    C. Initialize the variable.

    D. A variable does not need to be initialized.

21. What is a heap?

    A. A static allocation of memory

    B. A memory segment located within the CPU

    C. Memory that is swapped to the hard drive

    D. Memory allocation of a size and location that is assigned dynamically

22. What is the region in memory that is assigned to a process or a program when it is initiated?

    A. Cluster

    B. Stack

    C. Heap

    D. Pointer

23. What strategy does a local, caching DNS server use to look up records when asked?

    A. Recursive

    B. Iterative

    C. Combinatorics

    D. Bistromathics

24. What tool could be used to collect information like email addresses from PGP servers, Bing, Google, or LinkedIn?

    A. MegaPing

    B. nbtstat

    C. dig

    D. theHarvester

25. What would you use the program packETH for?

    A. Packet crafting

    B. Ethernet testing

    C. Man-in-the-middle attack

    D. IP analysis

26. Which of the following must be conducted first in order to hijack a session?

    A. Track the session.

    B. Desynchronize the session.

    C. Inject the adversary's packet into the stream.

    D. Disrupt the stream first and then inject the adversary's packet information.

27. Which standard advocates the Plan, Do, Check, Act process for implementation and validation of security controls?

    A. ISO 27001

    B. ISO 27002

    C. NIST 800-53

    D. NIST 800-161

28. Which of the following is used for recording key strokes at a terminal or keyboard using malicious software?

    A. Spyware

    B. Malware

    C. Key logger

    D. Recordware

29. Within SNMP, which of the following is used for authentication?

    A. PIN

    B. Asymmetric strings

    C. Community strings

    D. Cryptographic strings

30. What is the function of a CNAME record?

    A. Provides authentication to a website

    B. Encrypts DNS zone transfers

    C. Supplements an alias to a domain name

    D. Replaces the MX for security transactions

31. Software that creates pop-up advertisement messages while visiting websites is known as what?

   A. Adware

   B. Malware

   C. Pop-up blocker

   D. Freeware

32. The ability for information or services that must be accessible at a moment's notice is called what?

   A. Survivability

   B. Availability

   C. CIA

   D. Redundancy

33. What do you call a device that facilitates connections and acts as a middleman between user workstations and servers they communicate with, commonly outside the network?

   A. Firewall

   B. Main in the middle

   C. Gateway

   D. Proxy server

34. Which of these programming protocols passes objects between systems?

   A. SunRPC

   B. Portmapper

   C. RMI

   D. Nmap

35. Which of the following tools can be used to DDoS a target system?

   A. LOIC

   B. SIMM

   C. Cain & Abel

   D. AOL Punter

36. In SQL, which of the following allows an individual to update a table?

   A. DROP

   B. ADD

   C. COPY

   D. UPDATE

37. What type of attack would be used to collect authentication data between a station and an access point by forcing reauthentication?

   A. WEP cracking

   B. Rogue access point

   C. Deauthentication

   D. Handshaking attack

38. Of the following, which allows you to conduct password cracking?

   A. LOIC

   B. John the Ripper

   C. CPU Dump

   D. Wireshark

39. In the TCP/IP model, what is the equivalent of the OSI Network layer?

   A. Network

   B. Internet

   C. Transport

   D. Network Access

40. What flag is used to order a connection to terminate?

   A. SYN

   B. FIN

   C. PSH

   D. RST

41. Which of the following scanners provides ping sweeps and at times can be very noisy if not properly configured?

   A. Angry IP

   B. Cain & Abel

   C. `nmap -sT -T0`

   D. Nslookup

42. Which of the following is an application that provides ARP spoofing?

   A. Cain & Abel

   B. Evercrack

   C. Kismet

   D. John the Ripper

43. Which of these attacks targets the client in a web application?

    A. XML external entity

    B. Cross-site scripting

    C. SQL injection

    D. Command injection

44. Which option describes an adversary pretending to be someone else in order to obtain credit or attempt fraud?

    A. Impersonation

    B. Identity theft

    C. Masquerading

    D. Cloning

45. Which Linux distribution is best suited to support an attacker by providing the necessary preinstalled tools?

    A. Kali

    B. Security Onion

    C. Mint

    D. Ubuntu

46. If you were looking up information about a company in Brazil, which RIR would you be looking in for data?

    A. AFRINIC

    B. RIPE

    C. APNIC

    D. LACNIC

47. Which of the following organizations provides government-backed standards?

    A. EC-Council

    B. NIST

    C. CAIN

    D. NITS

48. You are performing an assessment on a cloud service that is the backend for a mobile application. What are you most likely to spend time testing?

    A. NoSQL database

    B. Data bus

    C. Microservices

    D. RESTful API

49. When you are attacking a web application, what server would you typically need to go through first to get to any programmatic content if the application is designed using a typical n-tier architecture?

    A. Web server

    B. Database server

    C. Logic server

    D. Application server

50. What does the Clark-Wilson model use to refer to objects when it is looking at integrity?

    A. UTC and CDI

    B. CDI and CTI

    C. UDI and CDI

    D. UTI and UDI

51. Which wireless mode is used when there is a point-to-point connection but no wireless access point involved?

    A. One to one

    B. Synchronization setting

    C. Ad hoc

    D. Clients must access a WAP

52. To sniff wireless traffic at layer 2, what must you have set on your wireless adapter?

    A. Transport mode

    B. Promiscuous mode

    C. Transparency mode

    D. Monitor mode

53. What is an advantage of a phone call over a phishing email?

    A. You are able to go into more detail with pretexting using a conversation.

    B. Phishing attacks are rarely successful.

    C. Not everyone has email, but everyone has a phone.

    D. Pretexting requires the use of a phone.

54. Which form of biometrics scans a pattern in the area of the eye around the pupil?

    A. Retinal scanning

    B. Fingerprint scanning

    C. Iris scanning

    D. Uvea scanning

55. Your biometric system at the entrance to your facility is having issues with a false failure rate. What is the most likely result of that?

    A. People having to change their password.

    B. Authorized people not being allowed in.

    C. The mantrap needs to be replaced.

    D. People stop using biometrics.

56. Why would you be most likely to use REST when developing a web application?

    A. HTML is stateless.

    B. HTTP is stateless.

    C. HTML is stateful.

    D. HTTP is stateful.

57. What steps does the TCP handshake follow as described by the flags that are set?

    A. FIN, ACK, FIN

    B. SYN, SYN, ACK

    C. SYN, ACK, FIN

    D. SYN, SYN/ACK, ACK

58. If you were to see the subnet mask 255.255.254.0, what would be the CIDR designation for that network?

    A. /24

    B. /23

    C. /22

    D. /25

59. On which port does a standard DNS zone transfer operate?

    A. 53

    B. 80

    C. 8080

    D. 25

60. What is the process of sending data to a device over Bluetooth without having to go through the pairing process called?

    A. Bluejacking

    B. Blueboxing

    C. Bluesnarfing

    D. Bluebugging

61. What UDP flag forces a connection to terminate at both ends of the circuit?

   A. RST

   B. FIN

   C. None

   D. URG and RST

62. What information does the traceroute tool provide?

   A. Username of the person logged in

   B. What links are encrypted on the network

   C. Layer 3 protocol details

   D. Route path information and hop count

63. What does the TTL value mean?

   A. The number of hops remaining until the packet times out

   B. The number of hops to the destination

   C. The number of the packets left

   D. The number of routing loops that are permitted

64. Which of the following indicates the authoritative DNS server for the zone being requested?

   A. EX

   B. NS

   C. EM

   D. PTR

65. Which of the following switches enables an idle scan within the Nmap tool?

   A. -Si

   B. -sI

   C. -Is

   D. None, because Nmap does not support idle scans

66. If you needed to enumerate data across multiple services and also store the data for retrieval later, what tool would you use?

   A. MegaPing

   B. Nmap

   C. Nessus

   D. Metasploit

67. What layer of the OSI model is the Network layer?

   A. 2

   B. 3

   C. 4

   D. 1

68. How does ARP spoofing work?

    A. Sending gratuitous ARP requests

    B. Sending gratuitous ARP responses

    C. Filling up the ARP cache

    D. Flooding a switch

69. A key that has to be known ahead of time to be able to encrypt data between two parties is known as what?

    A. Asymmetric encryption

    B. Symmetric encryption

    C. Pre-shared key

    D. Secret key

70. If you were to see `<!ENTITY xxe SYSTEM` in your logs, what would you think may be going on?

    A. XML entity injection

    B. Cross-site scripting

    C. Command injection

    D. Cross-site request forgery

71. What tool can be used to spoof a MAC address?

    A. MAC and Cheese

    B. Cheesy MAC

    C. GodSMAC

    D. arpspoof

72. Why might you use a phone call for a social engineering attack over a phishing message?

    A. Phishing attacks don't guarantee success.

    B. Pretexting only works over the phone.

    C. Pretexting is more detailed on the phone.

    D. More people have phones than email.

73. Which of the following encrypts community strings and provides authentication?

    A. ICMP

    B. SNMPv3

    C. SNMP

    D. IMAP

74. A wireless access point that looks like a known and legitimate wireless network may actually be what?

  A. Rogue AP

  B. Man in the middle

  C. Ad hoc solution

  D. Evil twin

75. Which of the following malware achieved a historical first by causing physical damage to a nuclear reactor facility?

  A. Stuxnet

  B. Blue's Revenge

  C. ILOVEYOU virus

  D. BackOrifice

76. You have found an SMTP server open. What SMTP command might you be able to use to identify users on that SMTP server?

  A. EXPN

  B. EHLO

  C. VRML

  D. VRFY

77. In a SQL injection attack, where does the attack actually execute?

  A. Web server

  B. Application server

  C. Database server

  D. Browser

78. What type of attack does POODLE invoke?

  A. Denial of service

  B. Man in the middle

  C. Distributed denial of service

  D. Credential harvesting

79. What is another name for Tor?

  A. The other router

  B. The onion router

  C. TLS open router

  D. Tunnel open router

80. In Kerberos, which of the following grants access to a service?

- **A.** Ticket-granting ticket
- **B.** Ticket authentication service
- **C.** Ticket-granting service
- **D.** Ticket granted access

81. What must a signature-based IDS have in order to be effective?

- **A.** An up-to-date set of rules
- **B.** A baseline
- **C.** Active rules
- **D.** Access to update user profiles

82. What type of attack is a Fraggle attack?

- **A.** XML entity
- **B.** False error
- **C.** Fragmentation
- **D.** Amplification

83. Who were the first ones to discover the POODLE vulnerability?

- **A.** Phil Zimmerman
- **B.** Akodo Toturi
- **C.** Urza and Mishra
- **D.** Moller, Duong, and Kotowicz

84. How many fields are there in a UDP header?

- **A.** Two
- **B.** Three
- **C.** Four
- **D.** Six

85. Which report would be best given to a client's senior leadership team?

- **A.** Analysis report
- **B.** Project summary report
- **C.** Executive summary report
- **D.** Chapter summary report

86. What is the security principle that might result in requiring two people to perform a single task?

- **A.** Least privilege
- **B.** Two-man source
- **C.** Biba Model
- **D.** Separation of duties

87. What tactic are you using if you are using the keyword `filename:`?

A. Footprinting

B. Doxing

C. Google Hacking

D. IoT device lookup

88. Why might you use Metasploit for a port scan over Nmap?

A. Metasploit supports more port scan types.

B. Metasploit stores results.

C. Metasploit is scriptable.

D. Nmap doesn't support port scanning.

89. As a network administrator, your manager instructs you to reduce the organization's accessibility to the file server. She claims that doing so will aid in preventing company trade secrets from being leaked to the public; however, you understand that doing so will have a negative impact on productivity and aggravate employees. Which part of the confidentiality, integrity, and availability triad is being impacted here?

A. Integrity

B. Confidentially

C. Least privilege/need to know

D. Availability

90. As a CISO, you published a security policy to your organization that a cross-shred shredder must be used to destroy classified documents in a secure manner. What type of security control did you implement?

A. Technical

B. Physical

C. Administrative

D. Controlled destruction

91. Which of the following is the most common network access translation type used?

A. S-NAT

B. PAT

C. Basic NAT

D. Public NAT

92. Due to the ILOVEYOU virus, Microsoft implemented a new business practice in its software to prevent such attacks from occurring again. What was it?

A. Disabling the macro features in Microsoft Office by default

B. Disabling the CD-ROM autorun feature

C. Setting user profiles to disabled

D. Removing HEKY_LOCAL_MACHINE\USER

93. If you needed to generate a message authentication code (MAC), what would you use?

   A. AES

   B. PGP

   C. SHA

   D. MB4

94. Which of the following denotes the root directory in a Linux system?

   A. `root/`

   B. `/`

   C. `home\`

   D. `\home\`

95. As the security administrator, you are tasked with implementing an access control strategy that will assign permissions to users based on the roles they will be hired to fill. What type of access control are you being asked to implement for your organization?

   A. RBAC

   B. MAC

   C. DAC

   D. UAC

96. As a black hat, you are conducting a reconnaissance operation on a potential target. You gather intelligence by using publicly available information, conducting stakeouts of the facility, and observing workers as they enter and leave the premises from across the street. What phase of the hacking methodologies are you operating within?

   A. Footprinting

   B. Fingerprinting

   C. Enumeration

   D. Passive reconnaissance

97. In Snort, which part of the rule dictates the source, destination, rule type, and direction?

   A. Rule body

   B. Rule action

   C. Rule header

   D. Rule connection

98. What prevents IP packets from circulating throughout the Internet forever?

   A. TTL

   B. Spanning tree

   C. Broadcast domains

   D. NAT

99. As a white hat, you are conducting an audit of your customer's security policies. You notice that the policies the organization published do not conform to its actual practices. You also note that the security administrators are implementing different corrective actions than what is supposed to be happening according to the policies. What is the correct action to take here?

   A. Inform the security administrators that they need to follow the security policies published by the organization.

   B. Recommend a once-a-month meeting that evaluates and make changes to the security policies.

   C. Allow the security administrators to tailor their practices as they see fit.

   D. Shred the old policies.

100. As an attacker, you are trying to prevent an IDS from alerting your presence to the network administrators. You determine that the rules that are set in place by the firewall are pretty effective and you dare not risk any more attempts to get past the security appliances. What is one method that may defeat the security policies set in place by the IDS and other security appliances?

   A. Firewalking

   B. Conducting a reverse shell exploit

   C. Session splicing

   D. Using HTTP

101. When a layer 2 switch is flooded, what mode does it default to?

   A. Fail open mode, where it mimics a hub.

   B. Fail closed, where nothing is passed anymore.

   C. Layer 2 switches process IP packets and not datagrams.

   D. Layer 2 switches cannot be flooded because they are collision domains.

102. Using Nmap, what switches allows us to fingerprint an operating system and conduct a port scan?

   A. -sS -sO

   B. -sSO

   C. -O -Ss

   D. -O -sS

103. What sort of an attack might you suspect if you had found an access point with the same name as an enterprise SSID?

   A. SSID scanning

   B. Evil twin

   C. Deauthentication

   D. Injection

104. If we send an ACK message to a system and there is no response, what can we determine from the port?

   A. ACK does not use a port.

   B. The port is open and ready to receive a SYN packet.

   C. The port is filtered.

   D. A SYN/ACK is returned.

105. Once the three-way handshake has been completed, in what state would a stateful firewall consider the communication flow to be?

   A. NEW

   B. RELATED

   C. ESTABLISHED

   D. STATELESS

106. If you wanted to use a browser plugin to identify technologies used in a website, what might you use?

   A. TamperData

   B. WappAlyzer

   C. GreaseMonkey

   D. Nova

107. IPv6 uses IPSec. Which of the following establishes the key agreement?

   A. IKE

   B. ISAKMP

   C. Diffie-Hellman

   D. TLS

108. What ICMP type denotes a "Time Exceeded" response?

   A. Type 3

   B. Type 0

   C. Type 5

   D. Type 11

109. Which of the following is a lightweight Cisco proprietary protocol for building security tunnels?

   A. EAP

   B. PEAP

   C. CHAP

   D. LEAP

110. What three services are usually included with the NetBIOS protocol?

    A. NBT, NetBIOS session, and NetBIOS datagram

    B. NBT, asymmetric session, and NetBIOS datagram

    C. NetBIOS datagram, NBT, and NetBIOS AD

    D. NetBIOS datagram, NBT, and NetBIOS SCP

111. What social networking site would likely be most useful for performing reconnaissance against a target?

    A. LinkedIn

    B. WhatsApp

    C. Facebook

    D. Friendster

112. What do wireless access points use to advertise their presence?

    A. Beacon frame

    B. Homing beacon

    C. Homing broadcast

    D. Broadcast frame

113. As a security administrator, you notice that your users are writing down their login credentials and sticking them on their monitors. What is an effective way of combating this security issue?

    A. Implement a PKI solution.

    B. Mandate password changes every 30 days.

    C. Set up a user and security awareness training session.

    D. Inform users that they need to memorize their credentials.

114. What does stateful inspection provide to the network administrator?

    A. It tracks all communications streams, and packets are inspected.

    B. It provides the administrator with a slower network response.

    C. It ensures that communications are terminated.

    D. It provides the administrator with reduced admin work.

115. As a white hat, you're tasked to identify all vulnerabilities possible on a network segment that your customer provided to you. You are provided nothing but a network identification, including an IP address and subnet mask. What type of assessment are you conducting?

    A. White box

    B. Gray box

    C. Black box

    D. Crystal box

116. What security property would you be addressing through the use of AES?

    A. Confidentiality

    B. Integrity

    C. Availability

    D. Non-repudiation

117. What type of network topology is being shown in the following diagram?

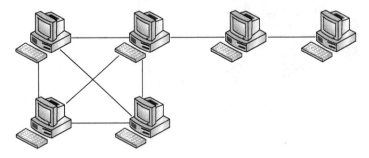

    A. Token ring topology

    B. Hybrid-mesh topology

    C. Bus topology

    D. Screen subnet

118. What type of subnet is being implemented based on this logical diagram?

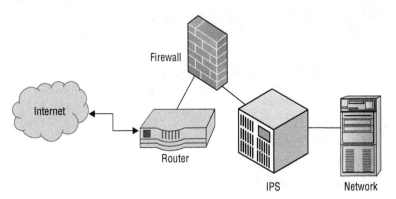

    A. Dual-homed firewall

    B. Double-screen firewall

    C. Screen subnet

    D. Screen firewall

119. What is missing from the TCP segment structure?

SOURCE PORT		DESTINATION PORT	
SEQUENCE NUMBER			
ACKNOWLEDGE NUMBER			
OFFSET	RESERVED	??????????	WINDOW
CHECKSUM			
OPTIONS		PADDING	
DATA			

A. Timing

B. TTL

C. ICMP

D. Flags

120. What would be the last values to complete the connection?

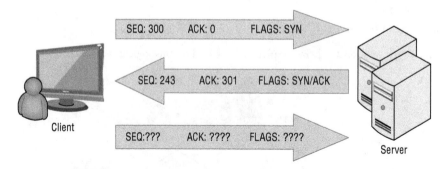

A. SEQ: 302 ACK: 200 FLAGS: SYN

B. SEQ: 302 ACK: 201 FLAGS: ACK

C. SEQ: 301 ACK: 202 FLAGS: ACK

D. SEQ: 301 ACK: 244 FLAGS: ACK

121. What type of application has impacted Ring 0?

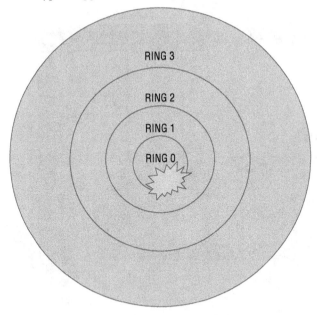

- **A.** Root access
- **B.** Malware
- **C.** Rootkit
- **D.** Trojan virus

122. What Bluetooth attack would allow you to make a call after gaining access to a device for the purpose of surveillance?
- **A.** BlueSnarf
- **B.** BlueSurveill
- **C.** BlueBug
- **D.** BlueBang

123. What type of attack is the adversary conducting in the following diagram?

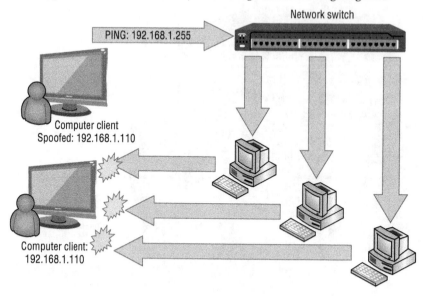

- **A.** Smurf attack
- **B.** Bluesnarfing
- **C.** Teardrop attack
- **D.** DoS attack

124. What type of attack is the adversary conducting in the following diagram?

    A. Man-in-the-middle attack

    B. Shoulder surfing

    C. Passive reconnaissance

    D. Foot inactive surveillance

125. In the following screen shot, why is the packet flag set to "Don't Fragment"?

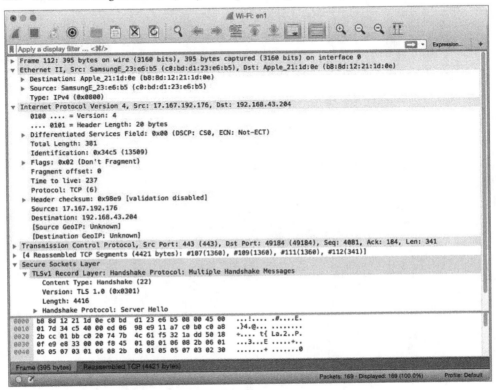

    A. The client is trying to establish a TCP handshake.

    B. A Hello Server packet has been crafted.

    C. The packet does not need to be fragmented.

    D. The client is trying to establish an SSL connection.

Chapter

4

Practice Test 4

1. Which of the following encryption algorithms uses two large prime numbers?
    A. RSA
    B. AES
    C. El Gamal
    D. RC5

2. What can be said about asymmetric encryption?
    A. The two keys are not related mathematically.
    B. The two keys are mathematically related.
    C. Both keys do the same thing.
    D. One key is shared between both parties.

3. What protection characteristics are in use with IPSec transport mode?
    A. The header is encrypted.
    B. Both payload and message are encrypted.
    C. It provides authentication to the sender's data.
    D. It provides encryption to the payload only.

4. Which of the following defines the private, non-routable IP address ranges?
    A. RFC 1929
    B. RFC 1918
    C. NIST 1918
    D. RFC 1921

5. Which DNS record maps an IPv4 address to a hostname?
    A. MX
    B. A
    C. AAA
    D. MR

6. What type of attack would you use if you wanted to gather passwords using the ticket exchanging protocol commonly used on networks that use Windows servers?
    A. EternalBlue
    B. Smurf
    C. Kerberoasting
    D. Rainbow tables

7. You are a disgruntled worker who is trying to access a blocked website at your job. You attempted to use a proxy server, but the website was blocked too. You then attempt to change the URL into another format that may not be blocked by the firewall, such as binary. What are you attempting to do?

    A. URL encoding

    B. URL obfuscation

    C. URL scrambling

    D. URL encryption

8. During an annual security training course you are facilitating, you place a call to another employee picked randomly who is not part of the training class. In this call, you state that you work in the help desk department and request their password in order to reset an account you noticed is locked. What risk are you demonstrating?

    A. Social engineering

    B. Weak passwords

    C. Malware being installed by workers

    D. Spam emails circulating the office

9. If you want to gather passwords from a Wi-Fi network, what technique would you be likely to use?

    A. KRAKEN

    B. BlueSnarf

    C. Evil twin

    D. Rogue AP

10. What key size range does RC4 use within WEP?

    A. 32 to 232 bits

    B. 16 to 40 bits

    C. 40 to 256 bits

    D. 40 to 232 bits

11. What command in Windows allows you to bring up a list of startup items, including their locations in the Registry or the file system?

    A. Mslookup

    B. MSConfig

    C. Regedit

    D. `iexplorer.exe`

12. How many stages are used in the handshake to establish credentials in WPA/2/3?

    A. Two

    B. Three

    C. Four

    D. Five

13. In SQL, what input value or term means *everything*?

    A.   *

    B.   ALL

    C.   SELECT

    D.   FROM

14. You are trying to black box test a web application, but it's being resistant to attack because of an authentication page at the top. What tool would you not use to find some direct access pages?

    A.   Metasploit

    B.   hping3

    C.   dirb

    D.   Burp Suite

15. In Kerberos, which ticket is presented to a server to grant access to a service?

    A.   TGS

    B.   KDC

    C.   TGT

    D.   AS

16. If you've compromised a system that has multiple network interfaces, what technique could you use to gain access to the other networks using the compromised system?

    A.   Kerberoasting

    B.   Trampolining

    C.   Privilege escalation

    D.   Pivoting

17. You are sending messages that are used to force a wireless station to continue to send messages to reconnect to the wireless network. What kind of attack is this?

    A.   Evil twin

    B.   Deauthentication

    C.   KRACK

    D.   Rogue AP

18. How many different techniques could you use to scan for open UDP ports?

    A.   1

    B.   2

    C.   5

    D.   10

19. What method is used to send a malicious URL using a text message?

   A. Smishing

   B. Vishing

   C. Phishing

   D. Whaling

20. What tool could you use on a Windows system to collect information about the Windows network, including the workgroup or domain you are connected to?

   A. ipconfig

   B. netstat

   C. MSConfig

   D. nbtstat

21. What type of attack might you use if you want to collect credentials by calling a user?

   A. Spam

   B. Social engineering

   C. Whaling

   D. Manipulation

22. Which of these would be an example of operational technology?

   A. Programmable logic controller

   B. Wireless access point

   C. Self-driving car

   D. Graphical user interface

23. What software technique tests for input values of programs and applications?

   A. Fizzing

   B. Fuzzing

   C. Obfuscating

   D. Encoding

24. What might be a quick and easy way to attempt to compromise a mobile device?

   A. SQL injection

   B. Buffer overflow

   C. Remote screen lock

   D. Smishing

25. At what stage within Kerberos is the subject authenticated?

   A. When the client presents the TGS ticket

   B. When the client receives the TGT

   C. When the client requests an ST

   D. When the client accesses the resources it requested

26. As a black hat, you are targeting a server room that contains important data. Which unconventional method would you use to DoS the entire room?

    A. Target the routers by DDoS.

    B. Conduct a Fraggle attack on the servers.

    C. Target the HVAC units.

    D. Change all the administrator login information.

27. What tool would you use to look for proof of concept exploit code on a system like Kali or ParrotOS?

    A. Nessus

    B. Zed Attack Proxy

    C. Searchsploit

    D. EDGAR

28. What tool could you use to easily create an executable that could be deployed on a system to connect back to a command and control system?

    A. msfvenom

    B. hping3

    C. ven0m0us

    D. OpenVAS

29. Which of these tasks would you not use the website Shodan for?

    A. Identifying webcams on the Internet

    B. Identifying industrial control systems on the Internet

    C. Identifying IP address ranges for a company

    D. Identifying default passwords on the Internet

30. What rotation cipher uses a matrix to map ciphertext to plain text and back?

    A. Caesar

    B. Vignere

    C. Rot13

    D. Rijndael

31. What is the purpose of dividing networks?

    A. To create larger networks

    B. To create more broadcast domains

    C. Ease of management

    D. To aggregate networks together

32. Who has responsibility for the operating system in a Platform as a Service (PaaS) offering with a cloud provider?

    A. Client

    B. Provider

    C. Both

    D. Neither

33. Which of these would be a very common vulnerability in cloud computing deployments that could lead to exploitation?

    A. Weak encryption

    B. Bad programming

    C. Lack of policies

    D. Weak access management

34. Which of the following is the highest classification level used by the U.S. government?

    A. Top Secret

    B. Secret

    C. For Your Eyes Only

    D. Confidential

35. What type of attack is being attempted if an application received ABABABABABABABABAB as input to a variable that had been allocated 10 bytes?

    A. Cross-site scripting

    B. Buffer overflow

    C. Heap spraying

    D. Command injection

36. What DNS record type is used to look up a hostname from an IP address?

    A. MX

    B. A

    C. PTR

    D. NS

37. What technique might a malware author use that would be most effective to evade detection by anti-malware software?

    A. Encryption

    B. Packing

    C. Compression

    D. Polymorphism

38. Which of these technologies would you use to remove malware in the network before it got to the endpoint?

   A.   Antivirus

   B.   Endpoint detection and response

   C.   Stateful firewall

   D.   Unified threat management device

39. What online database could you use to locate source code that could help you compromise a system?

   A.   LinkedIn

   B.   Exploit-DB

   C.   Metasploit-DB

   D.   Twitter

40. Which of these utilities would you use to capture passwords from the system Registry as well as from memory of a compromised system?

   A.   Nmap

   B.   LSASS

   C.   CryptCat

   D.   Mimikatz

41. What technique may be the most effective at compromising a mobile device?

   A.   Port scanning

   B.   App Store

   C.   Password compromise

   D.   Phishing

42. In the TCP three-way handshake, which is next after the initial SYN packet is sent?

   A.   An ACK is received.

   B.   A SYN is received.

   C.   A SYN/ACK is sent.

   D.   An ACK is sent.

43. Which attack would be less likely to be successful against a web application in a cloud-native application architecture?

   A.   SQL injection

   B.   Cross-site scripting

   C.   XML external entity

   D.   Cross-site request forgery

44. Which flag is used to terminate a connection that is only partially open?

   A. FIN

   B. RST

   C. URG

   D. SYN

45. Which character means NOT when defining a Snort rule?

   A. N

   B. !

   C. #

   D. %

46. What do NTFS alternate data streams provide?

   A. They can hide a file behind another file.

   B. They prevent a file from being changed.

   C. They prevent a file from being moved.

   D. They prevent an unauthorized user from viewing the file.

47. What protocol would you be most likely to use to get a system on your local network to send you traffic that should be sent to another system instead?

   A. SNMP

   B. SMTP

   C. FTP

   D. ARP

48. Which option describes the act of rummaging through trash to find important data?

   A. Dumpster swimming

   B. Social engineering

   C. Dumpster collection

   D. Dumpster diving

49. As a black hat, you forge an identification badge and dress in clothes associated with a maintenance worker. You attempt to follow other maintenance personnel as they enter the power grid facility. What are you attempting to do?

   A. Piggybacking

   B. Social engineering

   C. Tailgating

   D. Impersonating

50. Chris decides to download some music from a website while at work. When he opens the music files, a pop-up notification informs Chris that he must send $500 US to a PayPal account using the email address Shoju@scorpion.ru if he wants access to his system again. What do you think Chris may have installed?

A. Ransomware

B. Adware

C. Cryptoware

D. Trojan

51. What server configuration groups them together and provides redundancy and fault tolerance?

A. Clustering

B. High availability

C. Fault tolerance

D. Server redundancy

52. What type of label is given to a subject for security reasons?

A. Classification

B. Clearance

C. Secret

D. Confidential

53. What do you need to enable on a network interface that allows you to see the radio headers in the communication?

A. Promiscuous mode

B. Radio mode

C. Monitor mode

D. Capture mode

54. What mode on a network interface is necessary to capture traffic?

A. Promiscuous mode

B. Monitor mode

C. Capture mode

D. Interface mode

55. As a security administrator, your web application firewall logs show the following. What do you think is going on?

10; DROP TABLE users --

A. CSRF

B. SQLI

C. XSS

D. XXE

56. What is it called when you use a victim system as a router to get to other networks behind the compromised system?

   A. Piggybacking

   B. Social engineering

   C. Pivoting

   D. Auto-networking

57. On what default port(s) does SCP operate?

   A. TCP port 22

   B. TCP port 21

   C. TCP port 24

   D. TCP ports 21 and 22

58. Which key is used to encrypt messages to the owner of a certificate when using asymmetric encryption?

   A. Public key

   B. Private key

   C. Symmetric key

   D. PGP key

59. For an anomaly-based IPS to run optimally, what first must be determined?

   A. Updated signatures

   B. Accurate rules set

   C. Updated firmware

   D. Network baseline set

60. Which of the following attacks uses UDP packets to target the broadcast address and cause a DDoS?

   A. Smurf

   B. Fraggle

   C. Land

   D. Teardrop

61. Which tool causes sockets to be used up and can cause services to freeze or crash?

   A. Nmap

   B. Slowloris

   C. Cain & Abel

   D. John the Ripper

62. Which of these is a protocol might you expect to see used in an industrial control system to communicate with programmable logic controllers?

    A. SCADA

    B. Modbus

    C. SMTP

    D. SSH

63. What do you call the simple device that is used to manage the lowest-level elements of an industrial control system?

    A. Human machine interface

    B. Object

    C. Programmable logic controller

    D. ICS

64. What is a computing platform that provides a solution, hosted with a service provider, that customers could build applications on top of?

    A. Platform as a Service

    B. Software as Service

    C. FTP

    D. Web application

65. What is the act of looking over the shoulder of a victim to capture the information being displayed on their machine?

    A. Piggybacking

    B. Impersonation

    C. Shoulder surfing

    D. Shoulder peering

66. Which protocol has IPSec support natively?

    A. IPv4

    B. IPv6

    C. IPX

    D. AppleTalk

67. Which of the following is used to control and monitor the web communications of users to the outside world?

    A. NAT

    B. IPSec

    C. PAT

    D. Proxy

68. Which of the following allows networks to be subnetted into various sizes?

    A. NAT

    B. CIDR

    C. OSPF

    D. BGP

69. As a network administrator, you are tasked to separate different networks in order to increase security. By doing so, you attempt to create networks for users with a "need to know" policy. What can you do to ensure that only the workstations for those users participate in those layer 2 networks?

    A. Create broadcast multiple domains.

    B. Create VLANs.

    C. Maintain the collision domains.

    D. Implement a VPN solution.

70. At what layer does ICMP operate?

    A. Layer 2

    B. Layer 3

    C. Layer 5

    D. Layer 4

71. What is an easy way to gather credentials from wireless users?

    A. Deauthentication attack

    B. Man in the middle

    C. Evil twin

    D. Rogue AP

72. Why is address space layout randomization successful against buffer overflow attacks?

    A. Return address keeps changing

    B. Stack no longer exists

    C. Return address is wrapped

    D. Stack pointer moves

73. Which type of network uses a group of zombie computers to carry out the commands of the bot master?

    A. Zombie net

    B. Zombie group

    C. Botnet

    D. Bot heard

74. What protocol does the EternalBlue exploit make use of?

    A. SMTP

    B. RPC

    C. Kerberos

    D. SMB

75. Why would an attacker use a Trojan?

    A. To cause a DoS on a computer

    B. To delete files on a computer

    C. To encrypt the system

    D. To get a user to run it

76. Which of the following applications allows you to crack WEP passwords in a wireless network?

    A. Cain & Abel

    B. Wireshark

    C. Traceroute

    D. John the Ripper

77. What tool could you use if you wanted to identify directories that did not show up in the spider of a website?

    A. Wireshark

    B. DIRB

    C. Kismet

    D. Setoolkit

78. What tool could you use to fully automate a social engineering attack, like sending out a phishing campaign?

    A. Nmap

    B. Metasploit

    C. Setoolkit

    D. Aircrack

79. What tool could you use to assist in capturing radio headers on wireless networks?

    A. Nmap

    B. Ettercap

    C. Airmon-ng

    D. Ophcrack

80. You find the fping executable on a system. What was someone likely doing?

    A. Crafting packets

    B. Ping sweeps

    C. Port scans

    D. Exploiting a vulnerability in ICMP

81. Which of the following devices allows an attacker to collect all the data traffic with minimal effort?

    A. Layer 2 switch

    B. Bridge

    C. Router

    D. Hub

82. Which of the following describes a network appliance that acts as an intermediary server?

    A. Stateful firewall

    B. Packet filter firewall

    C. Proxy firewall

    D. Data server

83. With Platform as a Service, which of these would you, as a consumer of the service, not be responsible for?

    A. Application code

    B. Customer database

    C. Payment processing

    D. Operating system

84. What security property do you get from the use of a digital signature with email messages?

    A. Confidentiality

    B. Utility

    C. Non-repudiation

    D. Integrity

85. Which of the following algorithms successfully implemented the public key cryptosystem?

    A. AES

    B. El Gammal

    C. Diffie-Hellman

    D. RSA

86. What self-describing data description language might commonly be used to store or transmit information in a cloud-native application?

    A. YAML

    B. JSON

    C. C

    D. SQL

87. Where would you go to get the name and contact information for the administrator of a domain?

    A. DNS

    B. EDGAR

    C. RIR

    D. LinkedIn

88. A message that carries data and acknowledgments is called what?

    A. Segment

    B. Packet

    C. Frame

    D. Nibble

89. You have located an RMI server on a target network. What information would you want to get from that server?

    A. Development language

    B. Applications being hosted

    C. Developer identification

    D. Protocol being used

90. Which of the following is considered an AAA server?

    A. Kerberos

    B. Solaris

    C. Apache

    D. Exchange

91. What does a stack pointer do?

    A. It points to the next memory pointer in the stack.

    B. It points at the bottom of the stack.

    C. Memory does not use a stack pointer.

    D. It points at the top of the stack.

92. Apache OpenOffice and Microsoft Office have a built-in feature that allows the user to auto-mate a series of specified commands. These commands usually assist with daily routine tasks. This feature can be used in conjunction with launching malware. What feature is this?

    A. File sharing services

    B. Object Link

    C. Macro

    D. Compression

93. In virus scanning, what is the telltale sign of a virus?

    A. Hash value

    B. Signature

    C. Definition

    D. Trojan

94. When a security administrator is trying to reduce physical access to the backup vault, what type of control will they implement?

    A. Physical control

    B. Technical control

    C. Administrative control

    D. Logical control

95. What does a vulnerability scanner like Nessus not use to identify vulnerabilities?

    A. Exploited service

    B. Banners

    C. Application headers

    D. Vulnerability signature

96. What type of attack would you be conducting in a car using a laptop with a Wi-Fi card in it?

    A. Wardriving

    B. DoS

    C. Scanning

    D. War dialing

97. In Linux, how would you create a new user in terminal?

    A. `# useradd /home/samarea ssamarea`

    B. `>useradd raeleah`

    C. `cuser ray_j /home/ray_j`

    D. `useradd savion`

98. In Linux, what method uses a brute-force effort to locate a file?

   A. `find`

   B. `grep`

   C. `|`

   D. `search`

99. Which of the following would you not be able to access using an XML external entity injection attack?

   A. Internal web page

   B. File on the target system

   C. User cookie from the browser

   D. Network configuration

100. As a white hat, your customer asks what type of assessments you can conduct. What are they?

   A. Risk, threat, and vulnerability

   B. Malware, risk, and exploit

   C. Risk, vulnerability, and exploits

   D. Risk, mitigation, and vulnerability

101. A method that defends against a flooding attack and massive DoS attacks is referred to as what?

   A. Defense in depth

   B. Spam blocker

   C. Flood safe

   D. Flood guard

102. A firewall that blocks all traffic by default is known as what?

   A. Implicit allow

   B. Implicit deny

   C. Deny all

   D. Implicit prevent all

103. On which UDP ports does SNMP operate?

   A. 53

   B. 160 and 161

   C. 161 and 162

   D. 167

104. In IPSec, what is known as the security association manager?

A. IKE

B. ISAKMP

C. VPN

D. ESP

105. In WPA2, what AAA server can be used in the enterprise configuration?

A. RADIUS

B. Exchange

C. Solaris

D. NetWare

106. The act of falsifying data is also known as what?

A. Boink

B. Packet crafting

C. Spoofing

D. Data diddling

107. What would you use to inspect HTTP messages to determine whether there was attack traffic in the message so a decision could be made about whether to allow the traffic or not?

A. Stateful firewall

B. Anti-malware

C. Load balancer

D. Web application firewall

108. As a black hat, you are sending inputs to a web application to be sent to the LDAP server. What are you trying to conduct?

A. SQL injection

B. X.25 injection

C. LDAP injection

D. LDAP fuzzing

109. Which of the following allows the adversary to jump from the web directory to another part of the file system?

A. Directory traversal

B. Pivoting

C. Directory hopping

D. Directory shifting

110. When applications create variable memory segments in a dynamic fashion, what type of memory is being used?

   A. Stack

   B. Heap

   C. Virtual memory

   D. Virtual stack

111. As part of hardening a server, which of the following would the administrator want to configure prior to putting it into the DMZ?

   A. Disable unnecessary ports

   B. Open all ports

   C. Disable all accounts

   D. Reduce file restrictions

112. This fragment is found in web server logs. What kind of attack is likely to be happening?

   `&& cat /etc/shadow`

   A. SQL injection

   B. XML external entity

   C. Cross-site request forgery

   D. Command injection

113. What is a unique identifier that is used in Snort?

   A. SID

   B. ID

   C. PID

   D. NID

114. Which of the following tools can be used to steal cookies between a client and a server to use in a replay attack?

   A. Mouse

   B. Ferret

   C. Ratpack

   D. Nezumi

115. Which option describes the architecture in the following image?

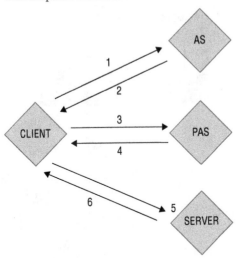

    A. Kerberos

    B. SESAME

    C. TACACS

    D. RADIUS

116. What type of operation is being conducted in the following image?

    A. Grant

    B. Create

    C. Take

    D. Revoke

117. What is missing from the following diagram?

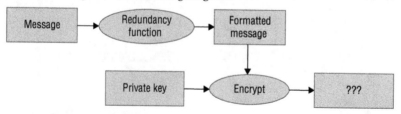

A. Signature

B. Plain text

C. Hash value

D. Ciphertext

118. What is missing from the following diagram?

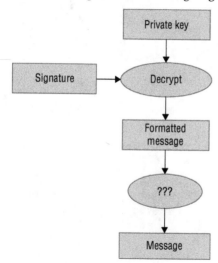

A. Verification

B. Hashed value

C. Digital signature

D. Public key encrypting

119. What would be the results of this XOR?

	1	0	0	1	1	1	0	1
XOR	1	1	0	0	0	1	0	1

    A. 01011000

    B. 10100101

    C. 10100111

    D. 10010100

120. What type of cipher is being depicted in the following image?

```
ABCDEFGHIJKLMNOPQRSTUVWXYZ
POULKJHMINBVYTREWQGFDSACXZ
```

    A. Caesar cipher

    B. Polyalphabetic cipher

    C. Monalphabetic cipher

    D. One-time key pad

121. What is the name of pointer that is missing in the following diagram?

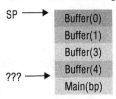

    A. SP

    B. HP

    C. MP

    D. BP

122. In the following screen shot, what sequence completes the three-way handshake with 23.253.184.229?

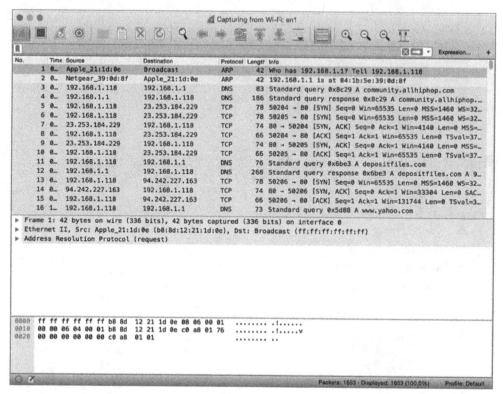

A. 5025

B. 1

C. 74

D. 64

123. In the following screen shot, what flag is set on frame 57523?

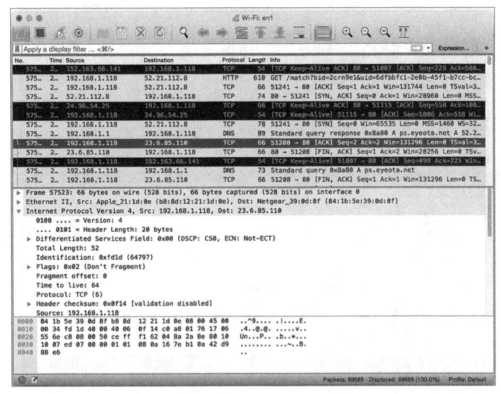

- **A.** 0x02
- **B.** 0x00
- **C.** 0x01
- **D.** 0x20

124. What tool could you safely use to perform dynamic analysis on a malware sample?
- **A.** strings
- **B.** Cuckoo Sandbox
- **C.** Ollydbg
- **D.** Cutter

125. As seen in the following screen shot, is the current connection vulnerable to Heartbleed?

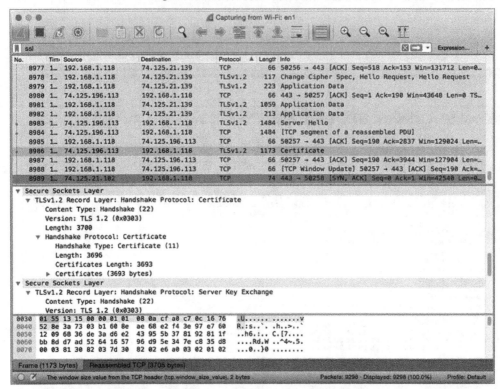

A. No. Heartbleed affects TLS 1.0.1 to 1.0.1f.

B. No. Heartbleed affects only SSL 3.0.

C. There is not enough information to tell.

D. Heartbleed is not the vulnerability; it is a heartbeat.

Chapter

5

Practice Test 5

1. When an attacker is querying for a number of services or login information on a target system, what are they trying to accomplish?

    A.   Enumeration

    B.   Scanning

    C.   Footprinting

    D.   Fingerprinting

2. Which of the following allows the adversary to obtain password information over the network in a passive manner?

    A.   Sniffing

    B.   Man in the middle

    C.   Password cracking

    D.   Account creation

3. Which of the following passwords will take the most effort to crack?

    A.   P@$$w0rd

    B.   Pass123

    C. $@($)!_

    D.   Thisismypasswordandnoonecanstealit

4. Where are logs located on Linux systems?

    A.   /home/log

    B.   /var/log

    C.   /log/

    D.   /home/system32/log

5. In Linux, which of the following accounts denotes the administrator?

    A.   Admin

    B.   Administrator

    C.   root

    D.   su

6. Which of the following is another name for NAT overload?

    A.   PAT

    B.   NAT+

    C.   NAT port

    D.   PAT overload

7. Which of the following is part of the overall portion of the SID?

   A. UID

   B. RID

   C. USD

   D. L5R

8. What is accomplished by a combination of ping sweeping and port scanning a target?

   A. Fingerprinting

   B. Footprinting

   C. Reconnaissance

   D. Identification

9. What response time measurement is used by default within the tracert program?

   A. Seconds

   B. Milliseconds

   C. Minutes

   D. None of the above

10. What is the encryption key length in DES?

    A. 64

    B. 128

    C. 56

    D. 80

11. Which of the following encryption ciphers replaced DES and was renamed AES?

    A. RSA

    B. AES

    C. Rijndael

    D. RC5

12. What completes the three-way handshake in the TCP connection?

    A. RST

    B. SYN/ACK

    C. ACK

    D. FIN

13. Using XOR, which of the following outputs a value of 1?

    A. 0 + 1

    B. 1 and 1

    C. 0 and 0

    D. 1 and 0

14. What would you use an intrusion detection system for?

    A. Blocking traffic

    B. Filtering traffic based on header information

    C. Generating alerts on traffic

    D. Logging system messages

15. Which of the following allows you to quickly search for websites that are vulnerable to SQL injections?

    A. Google Dorks

    B. Bing hacks

    C. Tracert

    D. 1=1'

16. What is the size of each of the fields in a UDP header?

    A. 16 bits

    B. 32 bits

    C. 8 bytes

    D. 16 bytes

17. The guest account under a Windows system has the RID of what?

    A. Not a RID, but a SID of 502

    B. RID 501

    C. RID 1001

    D. RID 1000

18. When trying to identify all the workstations responding on a subnet, what is the quickest method you might choose?

    A. Port scan

    B. Anonymizer

    C. Ping sweep

    D. Web crawler

19. What is the default port used for DNS?

    A. 80

    B. 22

    C. 8080

    D. 53

20. Which of the following tools can be used to crack passwords?

   A. Cain & Abel

   B. ToneLoc

   C. Wireshark

   D. WarVOX

21. Which flags would create a half-open connection if they are not responded to?

   A. FIN

   B. SYN

   C. SYN/ACK

   D. URG

22. Which tool can be used to query DNS?

   A. Twofish

   B. Cain & Abel

   C. WarVOX

   D. dig

23. Using Snort, which rule type allows for notification only if there is a match?

   A. Drop

   B. Alert

   C. Pass

   D. Block

24. Which switch in Nmap allows for a full TCP connect scan?

   A. `-sS`

   B. `-sU`

   C. `-FC`

   D. `-sT`

25. What type of control is a firewall?

   A. Barrier

   B. Administrator

   C. Logical

   D. Physical

26. Which of the following denotes the root directory in Linux OS?

   A. `\`

   B. `/`

   C. `C:\`

   D. `root/`

27. You call into the city manager's office claiming to be a part of the help desk team. You ask the clerk for her username and password to install the latest Microsoft Office suite. What type of attack are you conducting?

    A. Social engineering

    B. Piggybacking

    C. Masquerading

    D. Tailgating

28. You are driving in your vehicle looking for wireless access points to connect to. What type of attack are you conducting?

    A. War dialing

    B. Drive-by scanning

    C. Warchalking

    D. Wardriving

29. What is the process called when you're trying to inject bogus entries into the ARP table?

    A. Enumeration

    B. RARP

    C. ARP poisoning

    D. L2 dumping

30. What type of application design is being used if the application is written using nothing but AWS Lambda functions?

    A. Service-oriented

    B. Virtualized

    C. Serverless

    D. Infrastructure as a Service

31. An attacker was able to install a device at an unattended workstation and was able to recover passwords, account information, and other information the next day. What did the black hat install?

    A. Keylogger

    B. Key scanner

    C. Rootkit

    D. Trojan

32. What command has been used to display the network configuration in Linux OS?

    A. `ipconfig`

    B. `netstat`

    C. `ls`

    D. `ifconfig`

33. What directory holds the basic commands in the Linux OS?

    A. `/etc`

    B. `/bin`

    C. `/`

    D. `/config`

34. An attacker is dressed as a postal worker. Holding some large boxes, he follows a group of workers to make his drop-off in the back of the facility. What is the attacker trying to conduct?

    A. Phishing

    B. Sliding

    C. Piggybacking

    D. Shimming

35. What system element is used to store information and is installed by the web server?

    A. A text file

    B. Cookies

    C. HTML file

    D. XML file

36. You are walking around downtown picking up on open wireless access points. As you identify these access points, you place a symbol on a nearby building. What activity are you conducting?

    A. War walking

    B. Wardriving

    C. Footprinting

    D. Warchalking

37. What type of virus can change or rewrite itself every time it infects a new file?

    A. Polymorphic virus

    B. Metamorphic virus

    C. Trojan virus

    D. Shell virus

38. Which hashing algorithm was developed by the NSA and has a 160-bit output?

    A. MD5

    B. HAVAL

    C. DSA

    D. SHA-1

39. Aside from port 80, what is another common port used to connect to a web server?

   A. 8080

   B. 21

   C. 54

   D. 110

40. Which Nmap parameters utilizes the slowest scan?

   A. -T 0

   B. -sT

   C. -T 5

   D. -sX

41. Which of the following applications is used to inspect packets?

   A. Wireshark

   B. Cain & Abel

   C. Aircrack

   D. Nmap

42. What tool would make the most sense to use to identify IoT devices on a network?

   A. Postman

   B. Nmap

   C. Samba

   D. Cloudscan

43. How would an administrator set a password for a user in Linux?

   A. password user

   B. chmod pass user pass123

   C. pass user pass123

   D. passwd user

44. In Windows, what is the command to display the ARP cache?

   A. ifconfig /-a

   B. arp -a

   C. -a arp

   D. ipconfig /arp -a

45. Which application can provide DNS zone transfer information?

   A. Cain & Abel

   B. ICMP

   C. nslookup

   D. Domain Name Service

46. Which of the following is a top-level domain in DNS?

    A. `myserver.com`

    B. `.com`

    C. `http://myserver.com`

    D. `http://www.myserver.com`

47. Which is the second phase in the ethical hacking methodology?

    A. Reconnaissance

    B. Maintaining access

    C. Covering your tracks

    D. Scanning

48. What system uses a certificate authority?

    A. Realm

    B. SESAME

    C. PKI

    D. ICY Manipulator

49. Which site can you use to search through a database of vulnerabilities?

    A. `nvd.nist.gov`

    B. `google.com`

    C. `hackmybox.net`

    D. `breachthedoor.org`

50. As a business analyst, you study and collect information about your competitor using Google and the competitor's website and products. Which of the following best defines the actions you are performing?

    A. Google hacking

    B. Espionage

    C. Competitive intelligence

    D. Tradecraft

51. Which of the following relies on plaintext transmission when sending community strings as a means of authentication?

    A. SFTP

    B. SNMPv3

    C. SNMPv1

    D. Telnet

52. Which of following is a protocol that can be used with WPA2?
    A. RADIUS
    B. SESAME
    C. PKI
    D. Kerberos

53. A bank teller must have authorization with the bank manager to withdraw a large sum of money for the bank customer. Without the manager, she cannot accomplish the task. What access control is being performed in this scenario?
    A. Job rotation
    B. Separation of duties
    C. Multifactor
    D. Type 1 control

54. What does an exploit take advantage of within a system or network?
    A. Threat vector
    B. Malware
    C. A vulnerability
    D. A threat surface

55. Why would you use a RESTful design in your web application?
    A. HTML is stateful.
    B. REST is a reliable protocol.
    C. HTTP is stateless.
    D. REST is mandated by RFC.

56. In order for a wireless client to connect to an access point to gain access or be challenged with authentication, what information must be known?
    A. Key
    B. Username and password
    C. X.509 certificate
    D. SSID

57. What must a user have in order to sniff the full stack of wireless traffic?
    A. Wireless device set to promiscuous mode
    B. Wireless device that has 2.4 GHz and 5 GHz set to read only
    C. Wireless device set to monitor mode
    D. Ettercap set to clone

58. What command within the Linux OS can be used to delete files from a directory?

   A. del

   B. er

   C. -rm

   D. rm

59. Your company has been targeted by a series of phishing emails. In order to deter the attack, you quickly tell your users to verify senders. How do you go about implementing this?

   A. Ensure that the email is digitally signed.

   B. Call the sender and verify.

   C. Ensure that the email was not encrypted.

   D. Reply to their message and ask for their public key.

60. What cloud offering gives the customer the most responsibility?

   A. Platform as a Service

   B. Software as a Service

   C. Storage as a Service

   D. Infrastructure as a Service

61. What type of malware can be used to provide backdoor access to a system?

   A. Trojan

   B. Rootkit

   C. Root virus

   D. Spyware

62. Which type of software is considered a framework, a set of preinstalled tools, that aids in compromising and exploiting targeted systems?

   A. Cain & Abel

   B. Metasploit

   C. Mutavault

   D. Ettercap

63. What sets up a null session using Windows?

   A. `ftp ://yourdomain.com`

   B. `C$ \\yourdomain.com`

   C. `net use \\yourdomain\ipc$ "" /u: ""`

   D. `netcat yourdomain`

64. Taking binary code and converting it into a reversible ASCII string can be accomplished using what method?

   A. Encoding to ASCII version 2

   B. Hashing into MD5 or SHA-1

   C. Using Base64 encoding

   D. Converting to XML format

65. A city clerk received an email providing details about transferring money to a supplier. The email provides a URL asking for credentials for city bank accounts so payments can be made to the supplier. The email address does not match the one used by the supplier. What may be the issue here?

   A. Spear phishing

   B. Theft

   C. Whaling

   D. Tradecraft

66. Which of the following can be used to check for wireless signals?

   A. AirCheck

   B. Netcheck

   C. Ncat

   D. AirWare

67. Which switch in Nmap allows the user to perform a fast scan?

   A. -oX

   B. -PT

   C. -T4

   D. -sS

68. What flag is set to indicate data in the packet is a higher priority than other data?

   A. URG

   B. PRI

   C. SYN

   D. PSH

69. A user who is scanning for a network size of 128 nodes would use what CIDR?

   A. /24

   B. /25

   C. /28

   D. /30

70. An attacker uses a search engine to locate websites that are possibly vulnerable to SQL injections using special keywords known to the search engine. What search engine would they most likely be using?

A. Bing

B. Yahoo

C. Google

D. Whoami

71. A supervisor suspects that there are fraudulent activities being conducted in the workplace. What option can the supervisor employ to confirm their suspicion?

A. Duty rotation

B. Forced vacation

C. Installation of spy cameras

D. Installation of spy equipment

72. If a user wants to encrypt information using asymmetric encryption so keys don't have to be shared in the open, what would they use?

A. The receiver's shared key

B. The receiver's pre-shared key

C. The receiver's public key

D. The receiver's private key

73. Which record indicates the mapping of an IP address to a hostname?

A. MX

B. PTR

C. NS

D. CNAME

74. Which value is used in association with firewalking?

A. TTL

B. TCP

C. ICMP

D. Max hop count

75. A user side-loaded a popular app from an unauthorized third-party app store. When the user installed the app, it displayed a screen asking for payment and stating that if the payment was not received, the user would lose all access to data that was stored on their phone. What was installed on the user's phone?

A. Trojan

B. Spyware

C. Malware

D. Ransomware

76. Why would an attacker want to use bluesnarfing over bluejacking?

   A. Bluejacking sends while bluesnarfing receives.

   B. Bluejacking receives while bluesnarfing sends.

   C. Bluejacking installs keyloggers.

   D. Bluesnarfing installs keyloggers.

77. Which of the following is considered open-source information?

   A. Newspaper

   B. Trade secrets

   C. Information obtained from dumpster diving

   D. Information obtained from a man-in-the-middle attack

78. You receive a text message providing a link to a website with a message indicating you have vulnerabilities in your phone that need to be checked. What sort of an attack is this likely to be?

   A. Spear phishing

   B. Vishing

   C. Smishing

   D. Whaling

79. Which method would allow an administrator to reduce the threat of DNS poisoning?

   A. Increase refresh time rate

   B. Statically assign DNS entries

   C. Remove DNS entries

   D. Remove refresh time rate

80. Which Google hack allows the user to search for PDF documents that are located within a website?

   A. `filetype:pdf`

   B. `inurl:pdf`

   C. `typefile:pdf`

   D. `file:pdf`

81. Which hash algorithm produces a 160-bit value?

   A. MD5

   B. SHA-1

   C. SHA-256

   D. Diffie-Hellman

82. What standard format is used with certificate authorities?

    A. X.509

    B. X.500

    C. 802.1X

    D. PKI

83. In which method are two keys that are mathematically related used?

    A. Symmetric encryption

    B. Pre-shared keys

    C. Asymmetric encryption

    D. Shared keys

84. What key is included on a digital certificate?

    A. The public key is stored on the certificate.

    B. The private key is stored on the certificate.

    C. The key is not stored on the certificate.

    D. Both the public and private key are stored on the certificate.

85. An attacker gained access to your system and has collected your authentication credentials as well as a lot of messages you were sending to a colleague using your company's collaboration platform. What did the attacker likely install?

    A. Malware

    B. Virus

    C. Keylogger

    D. Key retriever

86. What type of scan would you use to map firewall rulesets?

    A. ACK

    B. XMAS

    C. NULL

    D. SYN

87. What is the default port used in POP3?

    A. 110

    B. 53

    C. 443

    D. 125

88. Which of these would not be a reason to use automation in a cloud environment?

A. Fault tolerance

B. Repeatability

C. Consistency

D. Testability

89. Which of the following has the best chance of alerting on previously unknown attacks on a network?

A. Signature-based IDS

B. Packet-based IDS

C. Behavior-based IDS

D. Rule-based IDS

90. If you were to ARP poison the default gateway, what would be the expected results?

A. You will receive traffic on that specific virtual local area network.

B. You will receive all the traffic on the current network associated with the gateway.

C. You will not receive any traffic.

D. You may cause a DoS on the network.

91. If you were moving your IT infrastructure from on-premise to a cloud service provider, what might you be most concerned about that would be different from what you have already?

A. Password complexity

B. No encryption

C. Application design complexity

D. Inability to implement security controls

92. Which of the following AAA servers provides asymmetric encryption?

A. Kerberos

B. RADIUS

C. SESAME

D. FTP

93. Which of the following tools allows some users to monitor all network activity?

A. Nmap

B. Metasploit

C. Wireshark

D. Netcraft

94. What is the default command port for FTP?

  A. 22

  B. 21

  C. 20

  D. 23

95. Which of the following are not objects in Active Directory?

  A. Users

  B. Computers

  C. Printers

  D. Files

96. Which of the following tools uses Metasploit to launch attacks like phishing campaigns?

  A. Setoolkit

  B. Ettercap

  C. Mimikatz

  D. Netcat

97. What tool could you use to discover previously unknown vulnerabilities in a network service or local application?

  A. Nmap

  B. Peach

  C. Mimikatz

  D. Rubeus

98. Which of the following will inform the user that the port is closed by the client itself?

  A. ICMP Type 3, Code 3

  B. ICMP Type 3

  C. ICMP Type 1, Code 1

  D. ICMP Type 3, Code 2

99. Which of the following layers in the OSI model contains the Transport layer in the TCP/IP model?

  A. Session and Transport

  B. Transport

  C. Network and Transport

  D. Data and Network

100. Which of the following encapsulates the header and the trailer?

    A. Data Link layer

    B. Transport layer

    C. Application layer

    D. Data Link layer with the logical link controller set

101. What program can be used to discover firewalls?

    A. Metasploit

    B. traceroute

    C. nslookup

    D. dig

102. Which of the following has no flags set and does not respond if a port is open?

    A. XMAS scan

    B. NULL scan

    C. Half-open connection

    D. ACK scan

103. Which of the following aids in fingerprinting a machine?

    A. Port scan

    B. nslookup

    C. dig

    D. The -sF switch in Nmap

104. Which DNS record type provides the port and services the server is hosting?

    A. SRV

    B. PTR

    C. SVR

    D. A

105. To establish a TCP connection, what must be sent first?

    A. ACK

    B. Hello packet

    C. Broadcast packet

    D. SYN

106. An X.509 certificate uses what value to uniquely identify it?

    A. Authentication number

    B. Serial number

    C. Private key

    D. Public key

107. Which encryption algorithm uses two large prime numbers factored together?

    A. El Gammal

    B. Diffie-Hellman

    C. RSA

    D. AES

108. Which is the initial value of the SID that is used to annotate an administrator's account?

    A. 500

    B. 100

    C. 5000

    D. 1

109. Which is the last step of the CEH hacking methodology?

    A. Maintain access

    B. Cover your tracks

    C. Scrub the logs

    D. Corrupt data

110. What file within the Linux OS contains administrative information about a user?

    A. /etc/shadow

    B. /etc/passwd

    C. /home

    D. /home/profile

111. What port number is used by NetBIOS for name services?

    A. UDP port 137

    B. TCP port 139

    C. UDP port 190

    D. None

112. Which rule type allows for logs and alerts in Snort?

    A. Drop

    B. Pass

    C. Alert

    D. Block

113. What protocol developed initially for serial connections may be used by ICS/SCADA infrastructure?

   A. SNMP

   B. Modbus

   C. SMTP

   D. XML

114. Which utility will display active network connections on a host?

   A. Netcat

   B. netstat

   C. Nmap

   D. Ns

115. What flag(s) is (are) set in the following screen shot?

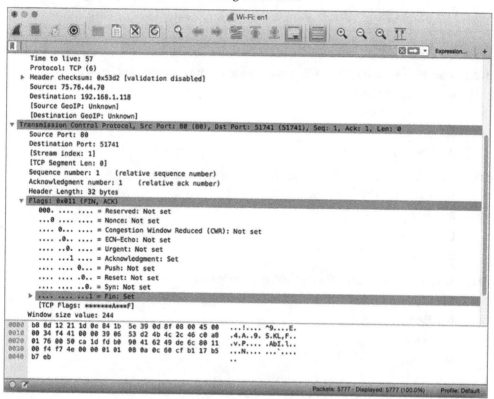

   A. FIN

   B. ACK, FIN

   C. ACK

   D. None

116. As shown in the following screen shot, what destination port is the current TLS connection being associated with?

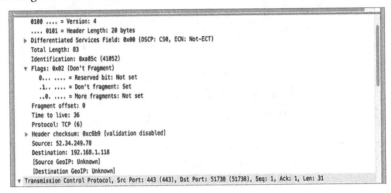

```
0100 .... = Version: 4
.... 0101 = Header Length: 20 bytes
▶ Differentiated Services Field: 0x00 (DSCP: CS0, ECN: Not-ECT)
  Total Length: 83
  Identification: 0xa05c (41052)
▼ Flags: 0x02 (Don't Fragment)
    0... .... = Reserved bit: Not set
    .1.. .... = Don't fragment: Set
    ..0. .... = More fragments: Not set
  Fragment offset: 0
  Time to live: 36
  Protocol: TCP (6)
▶ Header checksum: 0xc6b9 [validation disabled]
  Source: 52.34.249.78
  Destination: 192.168.1.118
  [Source GeoIP: Unknown]
  [Destination GeoIP: Unknown]
▼ Transmission Control Protocol, Src Port: 443 (443), Dst Port: 51738 (51738), Seq: 1, Ack: 1, Len: 31
```

- **A.** 51738
- **B.** 443
- **C.** 0101
- **D.** Not enough information available

117. What port is stackoverflow connected with in the following screen shot?

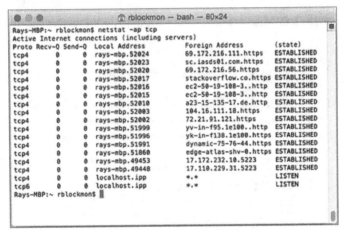

```
● ● ●              🏠 rblockmon — bash — 80×24
Rays-MBP:~ rblockmon$ netstat -ap tcp
Active Internet connections (including servers)
Proto Recv-Q Send-Q  Local Address          Foreign Address        (state)
tcp4       0      0   rays-mbp.52024         69.172.216.111.https   ESTABLISHED
tcp4       0      0   rays-mbp.52023         sc.iasds01.com.https   ESTABLISHED
tcp4       0      0   rays-mbp.52020         69.172.216.56.https    ESTABLISHED
tcp4       0      0   rays-mbp.52017         stackoverflow.co.https ESTABLISHED
tcp4       0      0   rays-mbp.52016         ec2-50-19-108-3..http  ESTABLISHED
tcp4       0      0   rays-mbp.52015         ec2-50-19-108-3..http  ESTABLISHED
tcp4       0      0   rays-mbp.52010         a23-15-135-17.de.http  ESTABLISHED
tcp4       0      0   rays-mbp.52003         104.16.111.18.https    ESTABLISHED
tcp4       0      0   rays-mbp.52002         72.21.91.121.https     ESTABLISHED
tcp4       0      0   rays-mbp.51999         yv-in-f95.1e100..http  ESTABLISHED
tcp4       0      0   rays-mbp.51996         yk-in-f138.1e100.https ESTABLISHED
tcp4       0      0   rays-mbp.51991         dynamic-75-76-44.https ESTABLISHED
tcp4       0      0   rays-mbp.51860         edge-atlas-shv-0.https ESTABLISHED
tcp4       0      0   rays-mbp.49453         17.172.232.10.5223     ESTABLISHED
tcp4       0      0   rays-mbp.49448         17.110.229.31.5223     ESTABLISHED
tcp4       0      0   localhost.ipp          *.*                    LISTEN
tcp6       0      0   localhost.ipp          *.*                    LISTEN
Rays-MBP:~ rblockmon$ ▮
```

- **A.** 42024
- **B.** 520303
- **C.** 52017
- **D.** 52020

118. As shown in the following screen shot, what is the TTL value?

```
●  ●  ●                    ⌂ rblockmon — bash — 80×24
Rays-MBP:~ rblockmon$ ping stackoverflow.com
PING stackoverflow.com (104.16.34.249): 56 data bytes
64 bytes from 104.16.34.249: icmp_seq=0 ttl=57 time=110.611 ms
64 bytes from 104.16.34.249: icmp_seq=1 ttl=57 time=23.498 ms
64 bytes from 104.16.34.249: icmp_seq=2 ttl=57 time=23.692 ms
64 bytes from 104.16.34.249: icmp_seq=3 ttl=57 time=23.303 ms
64 bytes from 104.16.34.249: icmp_seq=4 ttl=57 time=22.656 ms
64 bytes from 104.16.34.249: icmp_seq=5 ttl=57 time=24.136 ms
64 bytes from 104.16.34.249: icmp_seq=6 ttl=57 time=20.604 ms
64 bytes from 104.16.34.249: icmp_seq=7 ttl=57 time=23.487 ms
64 bytes from 104.16.34.249: icmp_seq=8 ttl=57 time=23.154 ms
64 bytes from 104.16.34.249: icmp_seq=9 ttl=57 time=23.145 ms
64 bytes from 104.16.34.249: icmp_seq=10 ttl=57 time=23.125 ms
64 bytes from 104.16.34.249: icmp_seq=11 ttl=57 time=100.855 ms
64 bytes from 104.16.34.249: icmp_seq=12 ttl=57 time=22.019 ms
^C
--- stackoverflow.com ping statistics ---
13 packets transmitted, 13 packets received, 0.0% packet loss
round-trip min/avg/max/stddev = 20.604/35.714/110.611/29.929 ms
Rays-MBP:~ rblockmon$ ▋
```

A. 128

B. 58

C. 64

D. 57

119. As shown in the following screen shot, at what hop did the user potentially encounter a firewall?

```
●  ●  ●                    ⌂ rblockmon — bash — 80×24
ms
 4  user-24-96-198-18.knology.net (24.96.198.18)  17.599 ms  10.577 ms  9.542 ms
 5  user-24-96-35-34.knology.net (24.96.35.34)  9.823 ms  10.642 ms  11.120 ms
 6  user-24-96-153-14.knology.net (24.96.153.14)  20.505 ms  28.997 ms  20.733 m
s
 7  dynamic-75-76-35-15.knology.net (75.76.35.15)  20.795 ms  21.908 ms  22.732
ms
 8  dynamic-75-76-35-73.knology.net (75.76.35.73)  27.340 ms  70.911 ms  26.862
ms
 9  de-cix.pat2.nyc.yahoo.com (206.130.10.78)  27.141 ms  26.498 ms  26.995 ms
10  ae-2.pat2.bfz.yahoo.com (216.115.100.74)  39.458 ms  39.941 ms
    ae-5.pat1.bfz.yahoo.com (216.115.96.65)  39.050 ms
11  et-0-0-1.msr1.bf1.yahoo.com (74.6.227.131)  34.942 ms
    et-19-1-0.msr1.bf2.yahoo.com (74.6.227.147)  37.867 ms
    et-19-1-0.msr1.bf1.yahoo.com (74.6.227.133)  37.238 ms
12  et-0-0-1.clr2-a-gdc.bf1.yahoo.com (74.6.122.17)  37.536 ms
    et-19-0-1.clr2-a-gdc.bf1.yahoo.com (74.6.122.39)  37.356 ms
    et-0-0-1.clr2-a-gdc.bf1.yahoo.com (74.6.122.17)  38.292 ms
13  po8.fab7-1-gdc.bf1.yahoo.com (72.30.22.45)  35.027 ms
    po8.fab1-1-gdc.bf1.yahoo.com (72.30.22.33)  43.781 ms
    po7.fab3-1-gdc.bf1.yahoo.com (72.30.22.5)  38.088 ms
14  po-12.bas2-7-prd.bf1.yahoo.com (98.139.129.195)  58.967 ms  42.345 ms
    po-16.bas1-7-prd.bf1.yahoo.com (98.139.130.1)  36.660 ms
15  * * *
```

A. 10

B. 14

C. 15

D. 19

120. What is the source address being used in the terminal output shown in the following screen shot?

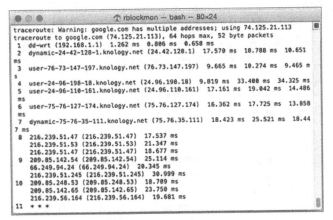

```
⬤ ⬤ ⬤                     ⌂ rblockmon — bash — 80×24
traceroute: Warning: google.com has multiple addresses; using 74.125.21.113
traceroute to google.com (74.125.21.113), 64 hops max, 52 byte packets
 1  dd-wrt (192.168.1.1)  1.262 ms  0.806 ms  0.658 ms
 2  dynamic-24-42-128-1.knology.net (24.42.128.1)  17.570 ms  10.788 ms  10.651
ms
 3  user-76-73-147-197.knology.net (76.73.147.197)  9.665 ms  10.274 ms  9.465 m
s
 4  user-24-96-198-18.knology.net (24.96.198.18)  9.819 ms  33.400 ms  34.325 ms
 5  user-24-96-110-161.knology.net (24.96.110.161)  17.161 ms  19.042 ms  14.486
ms
 6  user-75-76-127-174.knology.net (75.76.127.174)  16.362 ms  17.725 ms  13.858
ms
 7  dynamic-75-76-35-111.knology.net (75.76.35.111)  18.423 ms  25.521 ms  18.44
7 ms
 8  216.239.51.47 (216.239.51.47)  17.537 ms
    216.239.51.53 (216.239.51.53)  21.347 ms
    216.239.51.47 (216.239.51.47)  18.677 ms
 9  209.85.142.54 (209.85.142.54)  25.114 ms
    66.249.94.24 (66.249.94.24)  20.345 ms
    216.239.51.245 (216.239.51.245)  30.999 ms
10  209.85.248.53 (209.85.248.53)  18.709 ms
    209.85.142.65 (209.85.142.65)  23.750 ms
    216.239.56.164 (216.239.56.164)  19.681 ms
11  * * *
```

A. 74.125.21.113

B. 24.42.128.1

C. 192.168.1.1

D. 192.168.1.133

121. What would the server provide according to the following diagram?

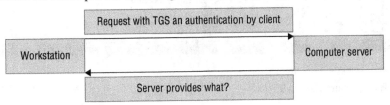

Workstation	Request with TGS an authentication by client →	Computer server
	← Server provides what?	

A. Server authentication

B. Key

C. Symmetric key

D. Access to client

122. As shown in the following image, who has both read and execute permissions for one object?

	OBJ 1	OBJ 2	OBJ 3	OBJ 4
SAVION	Read, write	write		execute
RAY J	execute		write	Read, write
SAMAREA	execute	execute	write	
RAELEAH	Read, write	read	Read,execute	

A. Raeleah

B. Samarea

C. Ray J

D. Savion

123. According to the following image, what browser is the user using?

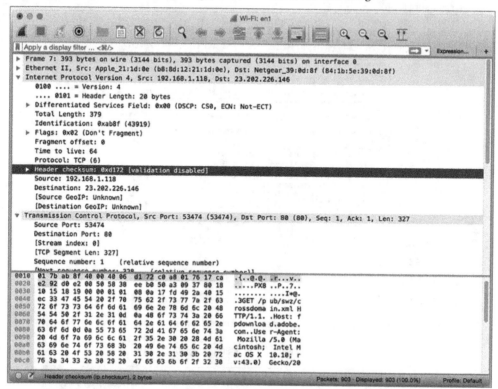

A. Google Chrome

B. Internet Explorer

C. Mozilla Firefox

D. Opera

124. As shown in the following screen shot, which of these provides the alias record under the members.tripod.com zone?

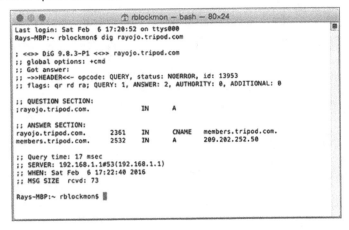

A. CNAME

B. A

C. rayojo.tripod.com

D. IN

125. In the following screen shot, what SSID is using the highest channel?

A. Rokugan5

B. Rokugan24

C. I can see you

D. Allen202

Appendix

Answers to Practice Tests

Chapter 1: Practice Test 1

1. A. Searching through the local paper is considered passive because it does not directly impact, alert, or establish any type of connection between the victim and the adversary. All the other answers involve directly connecting with the company or its network.

2. D. The Rijndael cipher was selected and then named the Advanced Encryption Standard (AES). 3DES was a stopgap to make it harder to decrypt DES messages while AES was being developed. Twofish and RC4 were not selected for AES, though they are encryption algorithms.

3. C. Storage as a Service offers the ability to store documents or other unstructured data, which could then be shared with others. Software as a Service keeps the data in the application, generally, and doesn't allow document sharing. Platform as a Service or Infrastructure as a Service could be used, but they would require additional work to allow files to be uploaded and shared. Storage as a Service would be the easiest and most likely.

4. D. An IPS has to inspect packets in order to match against rules written to look for malicious traffic. Both an IPS and firewall would typically generate logs. An IPS does follow rules and can drop packets, which is what differentiates the IPS from an IDS.

5. B. While all of the answers are true, the only answer that relates to security is option B, that IPv6 allows for header authentication. This ensures that packets have not been tampered with. This feature, Authentication Headers, is commonly thought of as part of IPSec.

6. D. Implementing an annual awareness training with the focus on social engineering will raise awareness in the organization. The training can be conducted by the information assurance section within the IT department. Ensuring patches are up-to-date is a good idea but won't prevent social engineering attacks. Host-based IDS may detect a social engineering attack but won't prevent it. The same is true for monitoring all email activity.

7. D. The attacker would edit and/or delete log information during the covering tracks phase, which is the last phase during the attack. Reconnaissance as well as scanning and enumeration are early in the process, followed by gaining access.

8. C. The attacker is using the Nmap function to conduct a TCP connection scan on the target, which is part of the scanning and enumeration phase. You would not use Nmap for either covering tracks or gaining access. You could use Nmap for enumeration, but you would typically need to run scripts to perform enumeration, which is used to get further details about services and users and other details about the target.

9. C. Unlike RC5 and RC6, RC4 is the stream cipher—it is the only symmetric cipher that uses streams. PGP is not an encryption algorithm. AES is a block cipher. ECC is an approach to encryption, allowing more computational challenge to key creation, but not an encryption algorithm itself.

10. A. Receiving a formal written agreement is critical because it sets the legal limit of what is allowed and not allowed to be conducted. It protects the pen testers from legal action if they stay within the agreed work performance statement. While all the other answers are excellent practices, they are not the most important practice.

11. C. AES remains the best encryption algorithm to use. It is flexible in its key size and economical in the computational power required. RC4 is a bad choice since it's known to be vulnerable to attack. MD5 is a hashing algorithm. Skipjack is an older encryption algorithm and wouldn't be the best selection here.

12. B. The SYN scan is used to detect open ports but does not complete the full three-way handshake. It is considered a "half open" connection. A connect scan does a full TCP three-way handshake to establish a connection. There is no such thing as an ACK connection. Many types of port scans could detect closed ports on a system.

13. D. The ARP request does not authenticate with the requested host; therefore, it is possible that the attacker can spoof the address of the victim with its own MAC address. ARP does not implement a username and password. You wouldn't use an ARP request as part of any DoS. Sending out messages to all hosts on a network is by design in ARP.

14. D. A brute force password attack is when the same username is tried with multiple passwords. There is no evidence here that any service is being impacted in a negative way, so this is not a denial-of-service attack. This is not an authentication failure attack. This is a credential stuffing attack, where the attacker uses known username/password combinations.

15. C. A man-in-the-middle attack is typically used to hijack a network conversation. This may be used to gain access to information, which may be of use in subsequent attacks. While a man-in-the-middle attack could possibly be used to gain access, that's not necessarily the reason for using it. Similarly, you wouldn't maintain access using a man-in-the-middle attack, nor would it be used to cover tracks.

16. A. Using SQL queries such ' or 1=1 is a way to get more information than should be provided through the application. This technique is used to test for SQL injection vulnerabilities. As this is about SQL, none of the other answers applies.

17. B. The default TTL value for most Microsoft operating systems is 128.

18. D. Using the 1=1 value in the URL will test for SQL vulnerability that would allow the attacker to assume that the web application can implement arbitrary commands. SQL test isn't an SQL query. The query admin and password likely wouldn't pass through the service-side program. The value || or |! isn't valid SQL and wouldn't yield anything of use.

19. A. SSH encrypts all traffic. If an attacker is using SSH, you wouldn't be able to see what they were doing, but that's not an advantage to anyone but the attacker.

20. D. The Ping of Death first appeared in 1996 because applications misinterpreted oversized packets.

21. C. Ransomware is the most impactful. It has cost businesses billions of dollars in recovery costs as well as lost productivity. While worms can be devastating, no worm has cost as much as the cumulative cost of ransomware around the world. *Virus* is a generic term. A dropper may be used to install ransomware, but it isn't impactful itself.

22. A. If there is question whether a Windows PC has been compromised, a sure way to see what processes are being executed can be found within the Processes tab of Task Manager. Programs such as iexplore.exe are legitimate; however, some programs such as !explore .exe and explore.exe attempt to look legitimate to avoid detection.

23. D. An evil twin attack is when an attacker uses a known SSID in order to lure unsuspecting users who would be encouraged to provide usernames and passwords that an attacker could then use to gain access to the legitimate network. A deauthentication attack is when an attacker tries to get a user to repeatedly reauthenticate in order to be able to crack the password. This is not a MAC spoofing attack because this not using ARP, and wardriving is when an attacker drives through a geographic area looking for Wi-Fi networks.

24. C. A checksum is a small-size datum that is computed against the message itself and creates its own fingerprint. It is a means of detecting any changes in the message itself for integrity purposes. If the two checksums of the original message and the received message do not match, the message has been compromised. A checksum serves as a validation that no errors occurred.

25. A. RSA uses 1,024- and 2,048-bit key strengths as asymmetric encryption algorithms.

26. B. Digital Signature Algorithm (DSA) provides only non-repudiation for emails. The others are encryption algorithms, which would not be used for nonrepudiation but would be used for confidentiality.

27. A. When a race condition occurs, either process may occur. If the timing is right, arbitrary commands may be executed with the current user-level privileges until the next process begins.

28. B. If you are able to ping and even visit an external website using its IP address and not its fully qualified domain name (FQDN), it is more probable that the DNS sever is having issues. While it's possible the firewall is blocking DNS requests, it's much less likely. Firewalls don't typically drop specific web requests, and it doesn't explain why you can ping an IP address but not its FQDN.

29. D. The most likely answer is that the new rules were poorly designed, so a lot of traffic was triggering the rules. There is no clipping level, and a switching loop would not be likely to generate a lot of alerts since it would be unusual to alert based on Spanning Tree Protocol messages. While a developer having local admin rights is a problem and could allow anyone who had access to the developer account to have an impact on the network, it's unlikely this is the source of the excessive IPS logs.

30. A. XSS is the only one of these attack types that target a client, the user's browser, in a web-based communication. The script in question executes within the browser (client). The other attack types are targeting the server.

31. C. When black box testing is performed, only the penetration testing team and a few selected individuals know about it. However, the penetration test team does not know anything about the target because this simulates a real-world threat against the company's network and incident response posture. White box testing means you have full knowledge of the network. Gray box testing is a mix of both white and black box. Blue boxes were used in the 1970s and '80s to obtain long-distance phone calls without paying. It is not a type of testing.

32. D. Although casing the target sounds right, the correct term for this activity is *reconnaissance*. In this phase, the attacker tries to gather all the facts they can about their target and answer any assumptions they may have through this activity. You are neither gaining access nor maintaining access if you are gathering information that could be used.

33. B. ncat is a useful tool, but it is not a scanning tool. ping and nslookup are very likely to be accurate, but Nmap is going to be the most useful. Neither ping nor nslookup is a scanning tool, though they could both be used within a script to do some forms of scanning.

34. D. While Nmap can't attack a system in the sense of providing any sort of access, the reason for using a connect scan over a SYN scan is to make the scan look more like legitimate traffic. It's possible that leaving a lot of half-open connections would be more suspicious.

35. B. Tapping a fiber line is very complicated. Unlike tapping into Ethernet, tapping into a fiber line could potentially drop network user traffic or even bring down the entire connection if too much light escapes the glass or plastic core.

36. B. Whenever you infiltrate a system, you would always want to cover your tracks by either editing or deleting your logs. This is important so the security administrators and investigators cannot trace your accounts, your location, and the methods you used to exploit the system.

37. A. Kerberoasting can be used to send requests using Kerberos with the intent of gathering information about accounts that could be used offline. This information would allow the attacker to gain subsequent access to those services. A man-in-the-middle attack is not a common attack type against Kerberos. The other two are not attacks against Kerberos.

38. D. Passwords are located in the Security Account Manager (SAM) file, which is located in C:\Windows\system32\config. You may be able to retrieve the passwords from the C:\Windows\repair folder as well, even though this folder may not be available.

39. B. During an XMAS scan, the adversary would receive an RST/ACK response from the port if it is closed because the scan sends the FIN, URG, and PSH flags, which is not a valid request according to the TCP RFC.

40. D. By encoding the payload, the adversary is trying to avoid IDS/IPS detection because it changes the signature of the original payload to a different format. Encoding may have some benefit, though encoding and encryption are not the same thing. If there is no port associated, the traffic won't pass through the firewall, so option C is a nonsense answer.

41. D. The longer the password, the more it uses the advantage of the key space for encryption. Short complex passwords can be cracked within a reasonable amount of time. A password that is simple but longer will be exponentially harder to crack. However, adding in additional complexity using different cases as well as numbers and symbols makes it less likely the attacker will be able to break the passphrase. A simple passphrase using no complexity may not get past a modern password cracking attack.

42. D. The adversary replaces the legitimate IP address for the fully qualified domain name with the malicious IP address. DNS does not make use of MAC addresses directly. Replacing one domain with another domain name doesn't make a lot of sense since the query response wouldn't match the query so the target wouldn't know what to do with the response. Replacing the victim's IP address in the query with the attacker's IP would only get the response sent to the attacker, not the victim.

43. C. With Cain & Abel, the adversary can forge certificates; however, the application lacks the ability to make the certificates look authentic. The user will be prompted, indicating that the certificate is not trusted.

44. D. The RC4 algorithm is used in WEP. Although RC4 is for the most part secure, the initialize vector is fairly short and therefore easily predictable. Cracking WEP is generally considered trivial today, which is why WEP has been discontinued. WPA is the preferred approach to protecting Wi-Fi communication.

45. B. The stranger is wardriving. Wardriving is the act of traveling with a high-powered antenna to pick up and use free or compromising weak Wi-Fi access points. Bluesnarfing is used against Bluetooth, and it generally requires closer proximity. Warflying uses drones, and brute-forcing a personal electronic device doesn't make sense in this context.

46. B. Model-view-controller is a common approach to developing applications for Apple devices. Microservices are not commonly used in a traditional application design. There is no such thing as NoSQL design. A RESTful API, NoSQL database, and microservices, especially if they are implemented in containers, suggests a cloud-native design.

47. D. When all the memory from the target server is drained, the server will not be able to process or store any information. This will eventually cause the server to freeze or crash, or it will possibly corrupt data. The end result is that none of the users will be able to use its resources. While a switching loop can cause problems in a network, it is not necessarily a denial of service and isn't an attack. A virus is not a denial of service either, necessarily. The same is true of forging a certificate.

48. A. If you look in the SAM file, after the username, the next value will be numerical. If it is a 500, this is the security identifier for the administrator account. The same security identifier is used on all Windows-based systems, just a 0 is used as the user id for the root user on Unix-based operating systems.

49. D. The American Registry for Internet Numbers (ARIN) is one of the five domain name registrants and is responsible for North and South America. There is no AMERNIC. LACNIC is Latin America and the Caribbean, not South America. RIPE has responsibility for Europe.

50. A. After identifying live systems, detecting open ports, and detecting the operating systems and IT services, you will then begin to scan for vulnerabilities. This will give you a list of potential targets you can exploit to gain access or gather additional essential information.

51. C. An ICMP Type 8 code is an echo request that is used within the Ping application. ICMP Type 0 is used for the echo response code. Destination unreachable is an ICMP type 3 message.

52. A. Ports 0 to 1023 are considered administrative ports because they require administrator-level access to listen on them. Higher-numbered ports are typically used as ephemeral, meaning they are used to assign source port numbers, which the server would respond to.

53. B. IPv4 used 32 bits for the address length, which was determined to be insufficient for the expected number of addresses of network-connected devices. As a result, IPv6 uses 128 bits, which is generally considered to be enough address space, as it allows for 3.4×10^{38} addresses.

54. A. The -O switch evokes Nmap to conduct an analysis of the target that is used to identify the operating system. The -sX switch performs an XMAS scan. There is no -sFRU switch, and the -sA will perform an ACK scan.

55. C. Using the command `net view /domain:<domain_name>` will retrieve all the systems that are joined to the domain. The `netstat` command is used for network information, including the routing table, which `netstat -r` will provide. The other `netstat` command provided as an option doesn't do anything. The correct syntax for `net view` is `net view /domain:<domain_name>`, not `net view /<domain_name>:domain`.

56. B. The man is conducting a shoulder surfing attack. By looking over her shoulder, the man is able to pick up passwords and any other sensitive information that she is using on her tablet without her knowledge or approval. Wardriving is an attack that looks for Wi-Fi networks in a geographic area. The other two attacks are not real.

57. D. An XML external entity attack (XXE) uses the SYSTEM facility in XML to gain access to system resources, including files, network resources or programs. As the fragment is XML, it is not a cross-site scripting attack, SQL injection attack, or command injection.

58. A. In a buffer overflow, data is written over memory that has been allocated for a function on the stack. This could cause several different outcomes, including data corruption, system crashing, freezing, and other untold consequences. While the program may crash from a buffer overflow, a crash won't allow for arbitrary commands to be executed. Heap spraying and format string attacks are different types of attacks and may not allow for remote code execution.

59. A. A proxy server is a middleman between the private internal network and the untrusted network. By initiating the connection, it can provide core protections associated with web exploitations. Routers and switches are types of network devices that don't sit in the middle of connections, merely passing traffic along based on source and destination addresses. A firewall will inspect certain properties of network traffic but not sit in the middle of the connection.

60. C. A honeypot is a server that is made to look like a legitimate target; however, it is configured to be vulnerable to an adversary's attack. The purpose is to learn about the adversary's methodologies of attack. While you may be able to easily exploit a target because patches weren't applied, it would be unlikely that there would also be a cache of readily accessible documents. Misconfiguration of either the firewall or web server would not explain this situation.

61. C. In Linux, the `lastlog` file is located in the `/var/log/` directory. This file contains information about users that have logged in. None of the other logs referenced here exists.

62. A. The Secure Shell (SSH) application utilizes port 22 to establish a connection by default. Port 21 is an FTP port, port 25 is for SMTP, and port 443 is the port used for encrypted web communication.

63. C. When you are conducting gray box testing, you have partial knowledge of the systems in play. White hat testing, while not really a thing in a formal sense, suggests you are doing good things. Gray hat testing also doesn't really exist, but suggests your motives are murky, not truly good but also not truly bad. There is no such thing as red hat testing. Red Hat is a company that maintains Linux distributions.

64. C. A next-generation firewall, sometimes called a unified threat management device, often includes multiple capabilities to prevent bad actors from getting into the network. One of these capabilities is malware scanning. A stateful firewall just keeps track of client state to make determinations about whether to allow traffic through. A stateless firewall can't keep track of state, and a web application firewall is used to identify attacks like SQL injection and cross-site scripting. It does not scan for malware.

65. D. Nmap is a tool that can be used to conduct scanning and other enumeration functions. It is capable of determining of what ports and services are functional and, to a certain degree, what operating systems are installed on the host. Cain & Abel is used to gather passwords. John the Ripper is used to crack passwords, and ping-eater doesn't exist.

66. B. There are no port numbers associated with IP because the addressing mechanism used there is the IP address. UDP and TCP both use port numbers as the way to address applications using those protocols.

67. C. Both IP and UDP are connectionless protocols. They do not form a connection-oriented bond between two ends. TCP is connection-oriented. FTP requires a user to log in before issuing commands and makes use of TCP, so you could say it's connection-oriented.

68. C. When data is being sent out from the corporate network, it is called exfiltration. While there is some evasion going on because of the tunneling, defense evasion is on the gaining access end of the attack lifecycle. There is no persistence or privilege escalation happening here.

69. B. Patch management requires understanding what the vulnerabilities are and then evaluating the patch for applicability before deciding whether to deploy the patch. You may also perform testing of a patch before full deployment to ensure no negative impacts. While the other answers may be good approaches to getting patches deployed, none of them can be truly said to be patch management.

70. B. FTP occurs at the Application level along with Telnet and other application services. The Network layer includes IP, while the Transport layer includes TCP and UDP. PPTP and RPC are commonly considered to be at the Session layer.

71. B. Nmap is a tool used for port scanning. Netcat is used to connect to remote ports or listen for connections on local ports. John the Ripper is a password cracker. theHarvester is a tool that can gather email addresses during reconnaissance.

72. A. Using the -sX switch causes Nmap to send packets with the FIN, PSH, and URG flags set. -sS is a SYN scan. -sT is a TCP scan, sometimes called a full connect scan. -s is the start of a command-line switch for a scan, while -x is not, so -xS does not initiate a scan. In fact, -xS does nothing in Nmap.

73. C. Nmap uses a database of known characteristics that best matches the target to determine the operating system. The fingerprint scan, in this case, is looking for the operating system fingerprint, based on a lot of information gathered by Nmap while performing port scans.

74. A. Cross-site scripting attacks the client side. SQL injection is a server-side attack. The other answers are not real things.

75. C. DNS, or Domain Name System, is an IP-to-name resolution service that utilizes port 53. Port 80 is used by web servers using HTTP. Port 8080 is an alternate HTTP port. Port 25 is used by SMTP for email.

76. B. The passwd file stores general information about the user's account such as name and location. The shadow file has the passwords on a Linux system. The other files don't exist.

77. D. Wireshark can be used to collect and analyze information in TCP segments. Nmap is a port scanner. SuperPing is a tool that can be used to send ICMP echo requests. Ettercap is used for spoofing network traffic for man-in-the-middle attacks.

78. D. The Fraggle attack uses a spoofed source IP and UDP packets as its method of delivery because of speed and lack of error correction.

79. D. The 0x90 is an instruction that tells the CPU to move to the next set of instructions in main memory. 0xGH is not legitimate hexadecimal. 0x99 is an add instruction. 0x91 is a duplicate instruction.

80. D. The Telnet client can be used to connect to arbitrary ports, regardless of the protocol they are talking. Once connected, you can send protocol commands specific to the application listening at that port. Those commands may provide banners you can grab. aescrypt can be used to encrypt files. Ettercap is used for spoofing attacks. netstat can be used for gathering a lot of network information. None of those can be used to grab banners.

81. D. Broadcast is no longer used within IPv6 because of its inefficiency. IPv6 uses multicast instead of broadcast.

82. B. A procedure is a step-by-step document that instructs the user to configure or set up a certain task or function. The result may be a baseline to build additional services on top of, but the step-by-step instructions are not a baseline. A technical advisory is a note that provides technical information but would not necessarily have step-by-step instructions in it. A guideline is a piece of information that should be followed but again doesn't have step-by-step instructions.

83. D. FTP uses port 21 for commands and port 20 for data control. Telnet uses a single port, port 23. ICMP does not have ports. HTTPS makes use of port 443.

84. C. MegaPing is a tool that has a lot of capabilities, including the ability to detect vulnerabilities as well as network scanning and DNS name lookup. It does not exploit vulnerabilities, however.

85. A. User account provisioning is a lifecycle program in which users are reviewed and granted need-to-know and least-privilege access and accounts are disabled or deleted. User accounts should be reviewed every 30 to 45 days to identify stale accounts. None of the other answers is a part of the account management lifecycle.

86. D. An individual who is dumpster diving is looking through the trash container hoping to score important information. The adversary is counting on people throwing away vital information such as trade secrets without proper disposal handling. This act can become potentially difficult to manage because it can be completely legal to do so, depending on the circumstance.

87. B. Ports 80 and 8080 are ports that are commonly used to connect to a web server. Port 80 is the well-known port for HTTP (web). Port 8080 is considered an alternate port and is used for web servers where the user does not have administrative privileges to listen on the lower-numbered port. Port 25 is used for SMTP, which is email. While port 443 is used for encrypted communications to a web server, port 53 is used for DNS. Ports 20 and 21 are used for FTP.

88. B. Although cloud computing is very versatile, it lacks the encompassing security posture one would think it may have. Because of the fact that you are depending on the commercial provider to enforce strict security practices and policies, you may actually never know what they are. One thing to keep in mind is that by using a free cloud solution, the contract that you agree to may very well provide cover for the provider from being sued by its customers for data loss, theft and damages, and other cyber incidents. With a LAN solution, the administrators have proper oversight and management. Administrators can strictly enforce proper security measures, provide incident response at a moment's notice, and notify the population of events in a timely manner.

89. B. While snoop and tcpdump are packet sniffers, they don't allow you to specify the fields out of a packet you want printed when a packet is seen on the network interface. Nmap is not a packet sniffer.

90. C. An object such as a file will have a classification level appended to it depending on its value and sensitivity level. The classification level is used to allow access to someone who meets or exceeds the clearance level of the classification and has a "need to know" requirement. Using classification labels is a method of implementing access control when dealing with sensitive information.

91. A. Cain & Abel allows the adversary or pen tester to carefully craft their own certificates or have the application create its own, depending on the scenario. In either case, when prompted to accept the certificate from Cain & Abel, the browser will warn the user that this certificate has not been verified (trusted). Nmap is a port scanner, while Ettercap is used for spoofing attacks. Neither of them will allow you to create certificates. Darkether is not a tool.

92. A. Vishing is when voice calls are used. Phishing uses email messages. Kishing is not a real thing. Smishing uses SMS (text) messages to initiate a social engineering attack against a victim.

93. C. Password Authentication Protocol (PAP) is a weak authentication protocol. It does not encrypt any data, and the authentication credentials are sent in the clear. There is no method for challenging at either end; therefore, it is very easy to intercept and masquerade as a legitimate user.

94. D. Multifactor authentication uses a combination of factors from something you have, something you know, and something you are. None of the other authentication types uses the something you are factor.

95. B. Whenever you are implementing more than one authentication factor, it is considered multifactor authentication. This means you are using two or more factors, such as something you have, something you know, and something you are. None of the other answers is a real thing.

96. A. MD5 is a hashing algorithm. It has no key associated with it, and therefore, it can be used by anyone. The purpose of hashing data is to provide a way to verify integrity, not origin. The other answers are all encryption ciphers, where a key would be necessary.

97. C. WPA2 uses a four-way handshake to establish the validity of both the client or terminal and the access point.

98. A. Kali Linux (formerly known as BackTrack) is an operating system that is widely used by hackers and pen testers alike. It hosts a suite of tools aimed at scanning, target enumeration, and exploiting vulnerabilities. Security Onion is commonly used on the defensive side. The other two options do not have security tools built in.

99. B. Antivirus software must be loaded with the latest virus definitions. Virus definitions are considered the DNA, or "signature," of known viruses. Without an updated virus signature in its database, the antivirus software does not know what new viruses are out in the wild. There is some anti-malware software that uses behaviors to detect malware on a system. There may be some effort required to administer a large installation of anti-malware software, but that's not a drawback, as any large installation of anything requires administration. Modern anti-malware does not consume a lot of resources, nor does it incur much in the way of performance impacts.

100. B. In the four-way handshake, a replay counter is used. This helps to protect against replay attacks, which could be used to allow an attacker to gain access to a wireless network. While WPA2 is used to encrypt, the purpose of the four-way handshake isn't to encrypt traffic. Neither multifactor authentication nor host checking is part of the four-way handshake.

101. B. The total UDP packet size is 65,535. You subtract 8 bytes for the UDP header size and 20 bytes for the IP header size, which is 28 bytes total. Subtract 28 bytes from the total size of 65,535. This should give you a value of 65,507 for the maximum UDP payload size.

102. C. Using LinkedIn can be a very good way to gather information about a target. Often, jobs are posted on LinkedIn, and they can include information about the target environment. Additionally, job responsibilities posted by the employees will provide similar information. While you might eventually use Nmap and even the -sO switch, it's probably not the best place to start. Calling the help desk to masquerade as a user is not likely to get you a lot of information used in the reconnaissance phase.

103. B. When the target has an open port and receives a packet with the FIN flag set, the target will not respond with anything. That is because the target knows that the sender has finished communicating. A RST is sent back from a SYN message on a closed port. A SYN/ACK is sent back from a SYN message on an open port. A RST/ACK is sent back to an ACK message that is not part of an existing connection.

104. C. Most modern switches are able to defend against such an attack. For those that cannot, the switch's content-addressable memory (CAM) will be flooded. This CAM table is where it learns the MAC address of hosts connected to its ports. When the switch is flooded with too many ARP requests, it will fail open and operate as a hub. This will result in all of the information being broadcast to all of the hosts connected to the switch. The adversary at this point can sniff LAN traffic.

105. D. The correct syntax to filter for a specific IP address is `ip.addr ==`. While you can also use `ip.src` or `ip.dst`, you would only get half the conversation. Using `ip` alone won't be a valid filter because it's not specific enough to tell Wireshark what you are trying to accomplish and you have to have `==` to indicate equivalency. Using a single `=` means you are setting a value, and Wireshark doesn't support that.

106. C. Smurf attacks make use of a broadcast address to send ICMP echo requests to, relying on large numbers of replies to overwhelm the victim. There are no longer any large smurf amplifiers, and most directed broadcast traffic using ICMP is blocked on the Internet. Fraggle is similar to a smurf attack, except it uses UDP. This is another attack that has been rendered mostly obsolete. A slowloris attack, though, may be successful against web servers since it relies on particular configurations and no protections in place in front of the web server. Many web servers may be vulnerable to this type of attack.

107. B. An example of spear phishing is an email soliciting the user to click a link or reply with sensitive information. Spear phishing targets specific individuals. Email phishing attacks would be sent to large numbers of people, potentially. While it is a type of social engineering, that doesn't capture the specific type of attack in use. While the final result of this might be identity theft, the information provided here doesn't guarantee that's the case.

108. A. A botnet is a collection of zombie computers that are used in concert to conduct a distributed denial of service (DDoS) on a target system. While you are performing a denial of service (DoS), that doesn't describe the network of systems that are used in the attack. Neither whaling nor social engineering are used to describe the network of systems used.

109. A. Physical controls are measures put in place to physically prevent someone from gaining access and entrance to a resource or a location. While a bollard is a physical barrier, a cipher lock is not. None of these is technical control or describes environmental design.

110. D. The X.509 standard describes what and how certificates are created. It includes the version of the certificate, serial number, who issued it, and the type of signature algorithm used. LDAP, or the Lightweight Directory Access Protocol, is an implementation of X.500. X.509 is a subset of the broader X.500 standard. X.509 certificates are used for public key cryptography, which is asymmetric in nature, not symmetric. X.509 is not a sandbox.

111. C. Steganography does not use encryption; however, it conceals or hides information within a picture or in an audio file. There is no key or encryption necessarily associated with steganography.

112. A. Data classification is used to identify sensitivity levels of information. Once data has been classified, it can be tagged in some way to ensure only the right people get access to it. Data masking is used to protect sensitive information, especially during application testing. Data encryption can protect sensitive information but wouldn't be used to ensure only the right people got access to that information. Data processing is a general term for working with data on computers.

113. A. The shared responsibility model determines who has responsibility for what aspects of a service with a cloud services provider. Bell-LaPadula is used for data classification and management. Carnegie Mellon Maturity Model is an old name for the Capability Maturity Model, used to assess maturity, especially within software development organizations. Ford, in addition to being a car manufacturer is a modeling agency, where live models can be hired.

114. B. The body that issues the Certified Ethical Hacker certification is the EC-Council. (ISC)² manages certifications like the CISSP. CompTIA manages certifications like the Security+. Microsoft manages a lot of different certifications, including the MCSE.

115. D. DHCP uses the User Datagram Protocol (UDP) because it is a connectionless service. IP is not a Transport layer protocol. TCP is connection-oriented and would slow down the DHCP process unnecessarily. ICMP is also not a Transport layer protocol.

116. A. The Internet Assigned Numbers Authority (IANA) is the authority from which domains receive their identification. In this case, it is noted as the IANA Registrar ID 292.

117. D. The process identification (PID) number is located in the far-left column. In this case, Terminal has a PID of 1186.

118. B. In a distributed denial-of-service (DDoS) attack, the victim is bombarded with attacks from multiple bots.

119. D. The missing label in the middle arrow is the SYN/ACK, which is part of three-way handshake. Without the SYN/ACK, a TCP connection cannot be established.

120. B. Under PID 0, the kernel_task is taking up 386 megabytes of memory from the system. This information is found under the MEM column.

121. A. The adversary who can successfully intercept and read traffic is conducting a man-in-the-middle attack. The purpose is to gain intelligence as long as possible without alerting the victim or IDS/IPS appliances.

122. B. The SYN stealth scanned 100 common ports, which is the most out of this particular Nmap scan.

123. A. The user's password file was hashed with SHA-512 and was salted. Using the salt function adds a pseudorandom value to the hashing algorithm that further secures and provides randomization to the output. This method adds another layer of security to prevent the hash from being brute-forced.

124. D. The owner has read and write privileges; group has read privileges; "others" have read privileges as well.

125. A. The TTL value is set at 64, which is normal for a Linux/Unix operating system. In the Ethernet frame, it shows the source as Apple_21:1d:0e, which now narrows our fingerprint to an macOS operating system.

Chapter 2: Practice Test 2

1. C. An administrative control usually consists of policies or directives that give the organization a general format to comply with. For example, a security policy may state that the only means to log into a workstation is through a common access card. An administrative control is also known as a soft control. An access control list is a technical control, while a mantrap and a biometric device are physical controls.

2. A. Using a /27, network administrators can successfully plan for eight different networks. A /24 would be a single network with a subnet mask of 255.255.255.0. A /25, since we are using powers of 2, every bit we add to or take away from the network prefix either multiplies or divides by 2 the size of the host portion of the address, the number of networks would be 2 for a /25 network allocation.

3. B. Telnet uses a default port number of 23 for connection and communication. Port 21 is used for FTP, port 53 is used for DNS, and port 443 is the port used for secure HTTP communication.

4. C. Diffie-Hellman, named for Whitfield Diffie and Martin Hellman, is a protocol used to exchange keys based on both parties in the key exchange mutually deriving the key. OAKLEY is also a key exchange protocol, but it uses Diffie-Hellman for the actual key exchange. AES is the Advanced Encryption Standard, which would require a key exchange but doesn't do key exchange itself. PGP is Pretty Good Privacy, which uses asymmetric keys. Because of this, the keys are managed without needing a way to secretly exchange them.

5. A. Digital Signature Algorithm, or DSA, is an algorithm that is used to provide digital signatures on files and email to provide nonrepudiation and authenticity. It does not provide confidentiality or integrity. AES is the Advanced Encryption Standard, so it would provide for confidentiality. RC4 is also an encryption cipher, providing confidentiality. PGP is a broader set of encryption mechanisms, which could be used to provide encryption.

6. C. The American Registry for Internet Numbers (ARIN) is the organization that tracks and records all matters that deal with Internet matters for North America and surrounding territories. It tracks IPv4, IPv6, and autonomous system numbers as well. ICANN is the Internet Corporation for Assigned Names and Numbers, used to manage IP addressing and port numbers, along with other information. APNIC is the Asia Pacific Network Information Center, which handles the same function as ARIN but for the Asia Pacific region. PIR isn't anything in this context.

7. D. Address Resolution Protocol, or ARP, is utilized at the Network layer because querying computers for their IP address is directly related to the Network layer in the OSI model.

8. B. A malware author would use obfuscation, meaning they would try to make the malware look different from something that may already be known by an anti-malware solution. Someone trying to understand what the malware did might use reverse engineering or disassembly to see what the code was doing. A dropper is a type of malware and wouldn't be used to avoid anti-malware since it could be detected itself.

9. D. The tool searchsploit will search a local copy of the Exploit-DB database for exploits and proof-of-concept code. While you can also search for exploits using Metasploit, you will only find modules in Metasploit and not source code for exploits that may not be available in Metasploit. Empire is a PowerShell framework that can be used post-exploitation. Nmap is a port scanning tool.

10. A. The Nmap program includes a large collection of scripts that can be executed when ports associated with the script are found to be open. Scripts provided as values for the `--script` parameter will be executed when the right conditions are met. These scripts can perform functions like identifying information about the Server Message Block (SMB) implementation on a target system. The only other answer that is valid in Nmap is `-sX`, and it performs an XMAS scan.

11. A. MegaPing is a GUI program that runs on Windows and can be used to perform ping sweeps and port scans. Ettercap is a program that will run on Linux, Windows, and macOS that can perform spoofing attacks. Dsniff is a collection of utilities used for spoofing. Nmap does have a GUI that could be used on Windows; the GUI is Zenmap. Nmap is the command-line program that runs under Zenmap.

12. B. The AES algorithm uses 128-, 192-, and 256-bit key lengths for encryption.

13. C. The exploit, developed by the NSA, that takes advantage of a vulnerability in the Server Message Block protocol is EternalBlue. Big Blue was long a nickname for IBM. The Shadow Brokers are the group that released the EternalBlue exploit, after stealing it from the NSA. WannaCry is ransomware that used EternalBlue as part of how it operated.

14. A. While attackers long used IRC as a protocol that could be used to manage botnets, businesses found that it was easy to just block all IRC traffic, which commonly used port 6667. Instead, attackers now use HTTP over common web ports like 80 and 443, because it's harder to block that traffic since it's used for legitimate purposes. While DNS and ICMP may be used by attackers to exfiltrate data from a network, they are not commonly used to manage a botnet. SMTP does not make a very effective protocol for managing botnets.

15. B. This policy is called the clean desk policy. It is widely used in industries where it's important to keep confidential and sensitive information secured by cleaning up before the workday ends. It prevents coworkers, cleaning crews, and other bystanders from pilfering and mishandling critical information. None of the others is a common policy used at organizations.

16. D. A local area network would be constrained to a small space, where you could run all connections back to a switch or, less likely, a hub. A wide area network would be used if the connections were, say, in multiple states or countries. A metropolitan area network is used for larger areas than a local area network but much smaller than a wide area network. This may be a network over a few city blocks, for example. There is no such thing as a mesh area network.

17. C. A web application firewall would operate at layer 7, which is the Application layer of the OSI model. A deep packet inspection may possibly operate at layer 7, but it's not guaranteed to since it may not understand the protocols being used at layer 7 and may just be looking at raw data. A stateful firewall is operating at layer 4 of the OSI model. Access control lists would provide a very rudimentary firewall and might operate at layer 3 or 4.

18. C. A common approach when using cloud-native design is to use microservices. You could use a monolithic design, but many businesses are migrating to the use of microservices, especially in a cloud provider's network, because of the management control provided to support microservices. While you could call the application n-tier by nature, you don't need to use a traditional n-tier model for an API. Additionally, the question was about the cloud provider space, which doesn't take into account the user component, which would be necessary for n-tier as well as model-view-controller.

19. C. *Impersonation* is a term that is associated with masquerading. It is not considered identity theft because it doesn't involve personally identifiable information (PII) such as Social Security numbers and birthdates. The attacker merely uses a means of communication such as a phone call to fool the victim into believing that they are who they say they are.

20. B. A rootkit is malware that embeds itself at the kernel level. It is extremely difficult to discover and remediate because the capabilities of the kernel and other operating system utilities are being used to hide the existence of the malware. While this type of malware may be associated with a worm, the behaviors described do not map to those belonging to a worm. A vampire tap is used to connect to network connections by piercing the copper wiring with small, metal spikes. The behaviors described do not belong to ransomware.

21. D. The NIST Cybersecurity Framework identifies the essential security functions as Identify, Protect, Detect, Respond, Recover. Plan, Do, Check, Act are the steps identified in ISO 270001.

22. A. A dictionary attack is the fastest method because the adversary has a file loaded with the most commonly used passwords. Because this file is finite in nature, this type of attack does not always work. For a guaranteed way of cracking an account, the adversary may resort to the brute force method, but this can take much longer than other methods, and in most cases, it's not even feasible. A brute force attack is more likely to work but is far more time consuming since the nature of a brute force attack is to try every possible combination, which requires that you know the length and the correct character set that the password uses. A birthday attack is about collisions and cryptographic hashes are not reversible.

23. C. The user identifier, or UID, is the designator that uniquely identifies each user on the workstation. GID is the group identifier, PID is process identifier, and SID is security identifier.

24. D. Using Nmap, the -sU switch command allows for the administrator to scan for UDP connections on a target workstation. If you receive an ICMP message of "port unreachable," it means that the port is closed or filtered. The parameter -sS is used for a SYN scan, while -sX is used for an XMAS scan. -PT is not an option used by Nmap.

25. B. A top-level parent is usually represented as .org, .com, .net, .gov, and .edu. Countries also have their own parent domains, such as .ru for Russia and .kr for South Korea. sybex.com would be a second-level domain, while www.wiley.com is a fully qualified domain name since it includes the hostname as well.

26. C. The output shows the client connecting to the address tuple 17.248.189.5.https, which is the HTTPS port at the IP address 17.248.189.5. The > in the tcpdump shows the directionality of the traffic. The HTTPS port is 443. Port 80 would be HTTP, and port 23 would be Telnet. Port 8080 is an alternate HTTP port, so would commonly be rendered as http-alt.

27. D. Although this is a denial-of-service attack and it could be distributed (not enough information to make that determination), it is specifically a SYN flood. You can tell because of the number of half-open connections, which means the attacker is sending spoofed SYN messages so no response to the SYN-ACK is possible, leaving the connection in a half-open state. A Smurf attack would make use of ICMP message.

28. A. A SPAN port on a Cisco switch is a Switched Port Analyzer. This is the type of port you would need to configure to gather traffic to and from another port where a user's system was connected. You could theoretically use a trunk port, but you would get far more information than would be useful, so it's not advisable. STP is the Spanning Tree Protocol, a protocol used to prevent switch loops in complex, switched networks. There is no such thing as a SPAM port.

29. B. Since you know the hostname and the system you want to redirect access to is on the Internet, you would use a DNS spoofing attack. This would allow you to intercept DNS requests, providing the rogue IP address in a DNS response before the legitimate DNS server could respond. Since you are redirecting access to a hostname, you would not use an ARP spoofing attack since that is based on MAC addresses. *Masquerading* is a common term for network address translation, which is not what we are doing. This is not a man-in-the-middle attack since you want to outright redirect traffic, not intercept and forward.

30. C. The module mimikatz, also available as a stand-alone program, can be used to collect passwords from memory. There is also a feature in Meterpreter called hashdump, not dump-hash, that can be used to dump hashes from the system password database. Autoroute relates to using a compromised system to pivot to other systems on the network. There is no module named siddump.

31. C. Whois.net is a free service that you can use to capture critical information for part of your footprinting when targeting a victim. Both nslookup and dig are used to gather information related to DNS, such as hostnames from IP address and vice versa. Ping is a utility used to send ICMP echo requests to determine whether a host is responsive on the network.

32. A. RFC 1918 covers IP addresses that are, by convention, not routable on the Internet. These are considered private IP addresses. The address specified in RFC 1918 are 10.0.0.0–10.255.255.255, 172.16.0.0–172.31.255.255, and 192.168.0.0–192.168.255.255.

33. A. The hping utility allows you to create packets effectively from scratch. These packets can then be sent out on the network to a target to see what responses come back, which may tell you a lot about the remote host. Ettercap is a program used to perform man-in-the-middle attacks. Nmap is a port scanning program, and pingcraft doesn't exist.

34. A. In most cases, a host-based intrusion detection system (HIDS) uses a signature-based detection method to protect the host. Most HIDS use a set of signatures that may be updated based on common threats. The problem with this approach is there will be a period of time between when a new attack is in the wild and when the signature has been updated.

35. A. In a PKI environment, the certificate authority (CA) is the subject that verifies a user's identity before issuing the certificate. This task may be delegated to a registration authority (RA), though it's commonly handled by the CA. A certificate revocation list is a collection of certificates that are no longer valid and shouldn't be trusted if they are presented. X.509 is the specification for a certificate and an organizational unit is a field in a certificate, as specified in X.509.

36. D. The method of cracking or breaking an encryption algorithm to discover either the key and/or the backdoor is called cryptanalysis. Brute-forcing is a type of attack where all possible values, say of a key, are tried. Cracking credentials might use brute force techniques, but this wouldn't be relevant when working on encrypted messages. Digital forensics is a field where details about a computer-based crime are collected.

37. D. Wireless networks come in two types—ad hoc and infrastructure. In an infrastructure network, there is an access point that all devices connect to. An ad hoc network is peer to peer, and there is no central device to connect to. The other answers don't relate to wireless networking.

38. B. In promiscuous mode, the network adapter does not alter any of the frames that it receives. It simply just copies the frames for analysis using a protocol analyzer such as Wireshark. Neither active nor stealth mode is correct or relevant for this. Carrier-sense multiple access with collision detection (CSMA/CD) is the way Ethernet operates to ensure messages can be sent over the wire.

39. A. The Counter Mode Cipher Block Chaining Message Authentication Code Protocol is an algorithm that uses a 128-bit key, which is based on the AES algorithm. 3DES and AES are encryption ciphers. LEAP is an authentication protocol, but not one used with WPA2.

40. D. In a Fraggle attack, the adversary forges the source IP address, which is the web server. The adversary will then ping the broadcast IP address, which causes all of the clients in that subnet to respond to the web server. This can cause a denial of service. A Smurf attack is similar but uses ICMP. While it's possible this is a DDoS, there is not enough evidence to suggest it's distributed. UDP does not use flags, so it can't be a SYN flood.

41. A. The final event in establishing the TCP three-way handshake is ACK. The three-way handshake in TCP follows the following pattern: SYN, SYN/ACK, ACK. The FIN message is used to tear down an existing connection.

42. A. You are using Software as a Service because Google is hosting the software applications. Platform and Infrastructure as a Service would be used to host your own web application. While you are also using Storage as a Service with Google's GSuite, the question specifically asked about email and document editing, which would make it Software as a Service.

43. C. Phishing is the process of sending email messages to users with the objective of gathering credentials or other information. However, a targeted phishing attack, such as the one where you want administrator credentials, would be a spear phishing attack. Pharming is the process of redirecting users to a bogus website that mimics a legitimate one. Man-in-the-middle attacks require that you intercept messages between the user and another systems.

44. A. IoT devices are just smaller, specialized versions of a Von Neumann computer architecture. As a result, they have memory, processor, and some sort of storage. They would not have a keyboard or other traditional I/O device.

45. A. Soft controls usually consist of policies, procedures, guidelines, or regulations that put in or recommend control measures for effective governance.

46. D. When a backdoor is installed, it allows the adversary to conduct remote call procedures such as a reverse terminal session or remote desktop procedures. The adversary can then conduct arbitrary operations as if they are logged in locally.

47. C. Biometrics is the method of collecting and using human characteristics such as fingerprints, facial recognition, and speech patterns in order to provide authentication for system access. A personal identification card would not collect or store physical attributes. Hair is not used for authentication purposes. Type 3 control is not correct and doesn't have meaning here.

48. C. Your voice; the pattern in your iris, which is the color pattern around your pupil; and your fingerprint can all be used to uniquely identify you. Your hair cannot be used for biometrics.

49. A. Digital Signature Authority, or DSA, uses asymmetric keys to provide non-repudiation. MD5 and SHA-1 are hashing algorithms. ECE does not mean anything in this context.

50. B. The inherent flaw in WEP is the IV, because it is only 24 bits long and transmitted in cleartext. Using a suite of tools called Aircrack-ng, you can successfully exploit the vulnerability in WEP's poor IV design. With sufficient data, WEP can be cracked easily.

51. D. Enumeration is the act of actively engaging the target system and gathering information. None of the others is something you would do during a penetration test.

52. A. Using nmap, the switch -sn disables the port scan, resulting in only ICMP echo requests being sent, and -O is the command to fingerprint the operating system. -sT is a TCP full connect scan. -V prints the version number of Nmap. -P by itself doesn't mean anything, and -Ps doesn't mean anything either.

53. C. POP3 is reserved for port 110. POP3 is a client/server protocol used to push email to clients. SNMP is port 161. RPC can use different ports, depending on the type of RPC. Additionally, the portmapper program is what listens for requests, redirecting messages to higher ports. LDAP is port 389.

54. D. dig is the command used to perform DNS queries, including address information from a fully qualified domain name. Ping is used to send ICMP echo requests to systems to determine whether they are responding. Nmap is a port scanner, and Hostcheck is not a real utility.

55. B. A virtual private network is used to allow remote users to connect to a business network as though they were directly connected. A VLAN is a virtual local area network, which is a way of breaking a large network into smaller sections. Segmentation is breaking larger networks into smaller networks. Isolation is a way of containing systems if they need to be kept apart from other systems.

56. A. Telnet is an application you can use to conduct banner grabbing. The Telnet client can be used to initiate TCP connections to any specified port, though the default port for the client to attempt connections to is 23, since that's the port for the Telnet server. Ping is used to send ICMP echo requests to systems. nmap -sP is no longer an option used, and del is the Windows command to delete files.

57. C. Giving the owner a list of vulnerabilities is the correct answer because patched systems, disabled accounts, and revoked certificates are objects that are already accounted for. They aren't going to be very useful in a report of findings.

58. C. IEEE 802.1X is the protocol for port-based network access that requires authentication. TACACS and Diameter are authentication, authorization, and accounting protocols.

59. B. Bonk uses UDP crafted packets to conduct a DoS on a Windows system. The UDP packets are oversized and when reconstructed can cause a crash on the target server. A Smurf attack uses ICMP. Smashing the stack is using a buffer overflow. Bonk is an attack that might work against very old versions of Windows from the mid to late 1990s.

60. A. A worm is self-replicating malware that does not need human intervention. It is a self-contained application, and it only needs to be introduced to the computer once to exploit the vulnerabilities found. *Virus* is a general term for malicious software. A Trojan is malware that masquerades as something legitimate. *Malware* is a general term, meaning malicious software.

61. B. The heap is the part of memory a program has access to for dynamic allocation. The stack is used as working memory for functions to store local variables. Stack smashing and buffer overflows return to the same thing: attacking the stack to run arbitrary code. Return to libc is an attack that uses a known address in memory for the standard C library to get arbitrary code to run in case stack smashing doesn't work.

62. D. A defensible network architecture allows security operations staff to monitor, detect, and alert on attacker activity as well as provide controls that can be used to isolate and contain an attacker once they are in the network. Defense in depth is a strategy for network design focused around preventive controls. A baseline configuration may be used in conjunction with an intrusion detection system. *Security measure* could potentially be used as another term for security control, which is a technology or process used to prevent or detect security events.

63. A. An SSO strategy could allow an adversary to conduct a DoS against the SSO service, making authentication and domain access difficult if not impossible until remediation occurs, which impacts many interdependent applications.

64. D. IoT devices often communicate with controllers on the Internet, sending them data or receiving commands. A commonly used protocol for this is HTTP since HTTP ports are usually allowed outbound from networks, where other ports may not be. Once connections are established from inside to outside the network, the controller can gather data or send commands. SMTP would be used for email and wouldn't make an efficient protocol for this activity. SNMP is UDP-based and would be harder to use to communicate with an IoT device from a controller. ICMP is used for simple control and troubleshooting and may be restricted outbound and certainly inbound to network devices.

65. B. By following the TCP stream using a protocol analyzer such as Wireshark, you are able to filter out the cleartext packets associated with a network communication. SSH and SSL are both encrypted. If you can capture plaintext passwords, you won't need John the Ripper, which is used to crack hashed passwords.

66. C. A content-addressable memory table, or CAM table, is a table that contains a list of MAC addresses that are associated with a port on a layer 2 switching device.

67. A. The most important task you have is to get informed consent. All of the other tasks mentioned are important, but for ethical reasons, getting informed consent is the most important.

68. C. Kerberos is a protocol that is used by Windows Server–based networks to allow workstations to authenticate against remote services. Diameter is an authentication protocol, but isn't used in this context. HIDS is a host-based intrusion detection system. SESAME is used for single sign-on.

69. A. Network address translation (NAT) is a process used for converting a private IP address to a public IP address when it leaves the LAN for Internet services. None of the other options is a real thing in this context.

70. D. Host IDS and network IDS are the only two types of IDSs. They are used to alert administrators about possible intrusions. They do not, however, prevent them.

71. A. The best place to go for financial information about a company, including financial reports, is the Electronic Data Gathering, Analysis, and Retrieval (EDGAR) system. HAL is the name of the computer in the movie *2001: A Space Odyssey*. MOLES is the name the computer named Edgar used to refer to the main character in the 1984 movie *Electric Dreams*. Google may lead you to that information, but EDGAR would be the most efficient.

72. B. The Health Insurance Portability and Accountability Act (HIPAA) is a federal regulation that mandates that all medical PII must be secured using encryption and other controls during transit and at rest. Failure to comply with the regulation can mean drastic consequences, such as jail time and heavy fines being imposed. PCI is used for payment cards, like credit cards. FISMA is the Federal Information Security Modernization Act and the PATRIOT Act is a wide-ranging law enacted after the September 11, 2001, terrorist attacks.

73. A. Time is one advantage the adversary will always have. They are on the offensive, and the more time they take to understand and develop their method of attack against the system, the more they increase their probability of success. The others may be beneficial, but victims have them on their side as well.

74. B. IEEE 802.1X is most associated with client authentication in wireless networks; however, it can also be used in an 802.3 environment. WPA is used for encrypting wireless communications. Radius and TACACS+ are used for authentication.

75. D. Using DROP in the SQL query causes the database to completely erase the corresponding table. In this case, the adversary who uses DROP TABLE Clients tells the SQL database to delete the table called Clients.

76. C. Nessus is an application that is used to conduct vulnerability scans against a target host or a range of hosts on a subnet. Snort is used for network intrusion detection, and Ncat is used to initiate and terminate network communications for arbitrary purposes. Metasploit may be used to scan for specific vulnerabilities, but it has a lot of other purposes as well.

77. C. The nbtstat utility is used to gather and show NetBIOS information on Windows systems. The netstat utility is used for general network statistics and information. Nmap is a port scanning utility, and Ping is used to send ICMP echo requests.

78. B. Phil Zimmerman created the Pretty Good Privacy (PGP) algorithm. At one point in time he was subjected to legal action by the United States government for not handing over the algorithm. Instead, Zimmerman published the algorithm on the Internet for anyone to use for free. AES and DES are encryption standards developed for the National Institute of Standards and Technology (NIST).

79. D. IPv6 has an address scheme of 128 bits. Due to its size, it can provide an IP address to every single person on Earth, with even more to spare. It also eliminated the broadcast protocol and implemented native features such as IP security.

80. B. A weakness in a system is a vulnerability. A threat being realized might use a vulnerability, but it is not a vulnerability.

81. A. Whenever a user climbs higher in an organization and retains and gains more privileges without being subjected to a need-to-know and least-privilege rule, it's called privilege creep. Administrators must constantly audit user access in their organization to defend against possible incidents.

82. A. *Node* is a general term for indicating a device that is connected to a network. It can be a computer, a router, a switch, a hub, or even a printer.

83. B. SNMP is the Simple Network Management Protocol, which can be used to remotely collect configuration information about a system. SMTP is the Simple Mail Transfer Protocol, HTTP is the Hypertext Transfer Protocol, and FTP is the File Transfer Protocol.

84. A. Meterpreter is an operating-system-agnostic interface to compromised systems that is part of Metasploit. Mimikatz can be used from Metasploit but is only used to collect passwords.

85. D. IKE is a protocol in IPSec that allows for two clients to exchange secret keys to establish a VPN connection.

86. A. The crossover error rate (CER) is the point at which the FRR and the FAR intersect. This means that the settings for the biometric device is set at an optimal setting for authenticating subjects. The false acceptance rate is the percentage of authentication attempts that are allowed through where the biometrics don't match. The false reject rate is the rate at which legitimate users are not authorized.

87. D. A Trojan is malware that is disguised to look like a legitimate application that is installed on a system. A rootkit is a type of malware that disguises its existence and often provides a backdoor for attackers. Adware is a type of malware that inserts advertisements on a victim's computer. Spyware has been used to provide details about a user's actions to an attacker.

88. C. Secure FTP uses TCP port 22, which is also utilized by Secure Shell (SSH). This is the preferred method of file transit if security is a concern.

89. A. Rainbow tables use precomputed hashes, which consume disk space. The more hashes you have, which would increase the success rate, the more disk space you use. This type of password cracking is low on processor utilization compared with a cracking technique like brute force.

90. B. This is likely a phishing attack since it takes place via email. Smishing uses text messages, and vishing uses voice messages. Fishing is used to catch fish, not usernames and passwords.

91. A. LDAP, which is the Lightweight Directory Access Protocol, uses port 389. Microsoft Active Directory-Directory Service uses LDAP in this manner. IMAP uses port 143. SMB and RPC use multiple ports.

92. B. The certificate authority is the system responsible for creating certificates and signing them on behalf of the subject requesting it. A registration authority is an optional system in a public key infrastructure that could be used to validate a user's identity prior to issuing a certificate. The other two are not parts of a public key infrastructure for the issuance and management of certificates.

93. B. While you can most efficiently use role-based access control to implement this, the principle of least privilege is used to ensure users have just the level of access they need and no more.

94. D. Macros should be disabled because they can be used to execute arbitrary code that can be malicious, such as a macro virus.

95. C. An escrow is a place to store certificates and keys in case the primary source of the key or certificate is unavailable. An example of this is the use of Active Directory to store keys in case a user loses theirs or the organization needs to gain access to the keys.

96. A. HTTPS uses the standard port 443 for browsing the Internet with encryption. Port 8080 is an alternate port for HTTP. Port 80 is the standard port for HTTP, without encryption. Port 22 is the port used for SSH.

97. D. Single sign-on (SSO) is a method used to allow users to authenticate once and have access to multiple resources. If it's not used, the user would have to continuously enter their credentials to get access to resources, which can be cumbersome. Kerberos may handle this transparently for users, but the term for the process is *single sign-on*. The other two options are made up.

98. B. A router is used to separate broadcast domains. This allows a single router to have multiple networks and keeps network traffic at a minimum. On a broadcast domain, all communication is handled locally, from MAC address to MAC address. Once a MAC address is not on the local network, it requires a router to transit the layer 3 boundary, using IP addresses to send traffic to.

99. D. The traceroute program works by setting the time to live (TTL) at 1, waiting to receive the time exceeded in transit message. The source of that message is the first hop. It then increments the TTL to 2 and so on until it receives either a port or host unreachable message, indicating it has reached the end of the trace. The message that allows the program to know each individual hop, though, is the time exceeded in transit message.

100. C. Each layer of the OSI model has a name for the collection of data encapsulated within that layer. This is called the protocol data unit (PDU). Layer 2 is the frame, layer 3 is the packet, and layer 4 is either the segment or datagram, depending on whether you are referring to a UDP or TCP message. As UDP is the user datagram protocol, the PDU for UDP is called a datagram. TCP uses segments.

101. D. The SAM file is the object that contains the list of password hashes for users who reside on the current system. It contains the user account information along with their security identification (SID). None of the other filenames is correct.

102. A. Brute-forcing is a method used to try every single combination of letters, numbers, and special characters to determine a password. It is the only method that will absolutely work. Pass the hash is a technique that collects a hash used to authenticate and passes it along to another system where it can be accepted. A dictionary attack uses known hash values, and social engineering is used to just outright ask for the password, commonly.

103. B. The sum of the binaries for read, write, and execute is 7. The owner, group, and others would each receive a numeral 7 to indicate read, write, and execute privileges on a target object. The permissions use the following values: read is 4, write is 2, execute is 1. If you add those values together, you get 7. If you want to know the numeric value for any permission set, just add the numbers associated with individual permissions. Read and execute, for instance, would be 4 + 1, or 5.

104. C. Data that has been corrupted, regardless of how it was corrupted, has lost its integrity. You might argue there is also an issue with availability since the clean data is no longer there to use, but the reason for that is a problem of integrity.

105. A. Metasploit is considered a framework for pen testing. There are many different ways to accomplish a certain task that a pen tester or an adversary may use against a target system or a network. Cain & Abel is used to crack passwords, Nessus is used to scan for vulnerabilities and Security Onion is a defensive-oriented Linux distribution.

106. D. Using the attribute command `attrib` plus the switch that signifies to hide, +h, you would type the name of the file you want to hide. It is then only accessible to the owner of the file at that point. Another option is to open the file's properties and toggle the Hidden check box as well.

107. A. The MAC address has six octets for the address and a range from 0 to 9 and A to F. Option A is the only answer where there are six octets, and they follow hexadecimal numbering principles (0–9, A–F).

108. B. A stateful firewall would operate at layer 4 of the OSI model, since it keeps track of the state of connections based on the port and IP address tuple. An application firewall would be layer 7.

109. A. A SYN scan uses half-open connections, meaning the scanner waits to receive either a SYN/ACK if the port is open or a RST if the port is closed. Once it gets that, it tears the connection down. This means there may be a lot of half-open connections showing up on a target. SYN scans are very accurate. A SYN scan does not complete the connection, and while SYN scans may be blocked by a security device, firewalls do not block all SYN messages.

110. B. Anti-malware software is a great tool; however, if a system is infected with a zero-day exploit or virus, the anti-malware will not be able to defend against it because it does not recognize the malware signature.

111. A. The algorithm that was eventually chosen as the Advanced Encryption Standard (AES) was Rijdael. Lucifer was the original name of the algorithm selected to be the Data Encryption Standard (DES). The other two are both related to encryption but are not correct answers.

112. B. The process used to convert opcodes back to assembly language, which are mnemonics more easily read by humans, is disassembly. Decompilation takes a compiled program and attempts to restore it to source code, which is a higher level than assembly language. Decryption is used to take ciphertext and return it to plain text.

113. B. Ransomware is a type of malware that encrypts the target system. It then asks the victim to send money to receive the key to unlock their system.

114. C. Wireshark has the ability to decrypt encrypted messages if it is provided the keys associated with a certificate.

115. A. Public key infrastructure (PKI) uses certificate authorities (CAs) and registration authorities (RAs) to validate, sign, and issue certificates to users in their domain.

116. B. Under the Ethernet (layer 2 header), the sender is broadcasting an ARP request.

117. B. Under the EN1, the IP address is given as 192.168.1.118, and it has a broadcast address of 192.168.1.255.

118. D. When you are observing the file source on a web page, the `meta charset` will show what encoding type is being used. In this case, it is using the UTF-8 encode method.

119. A. In the SSL header, the TLS version is determined to be 1.2 after the security association was reestablished.

120. C. Entering certain characters such as an ' or 1=1 can provide clues about whether a website is vulnerable to SQL injection. In this case, we received an error from the SQL database, which means it is vulnerable to SQL injection.

121. B. The adversary in this case in trying to redirect their position from the web server to the actual file system itself. Using the `cmd.exe` application, they are trying to gain access to the Windows terminal for arbitrary command execution.

122. A. In the Domain Name System section, you can determine that `www.google.com` is being used as a DNS resolution for this scenario.

123. C. The `/etc/passwd` file does not show the passwords for the accounts on the system. Passwords are stored in the `/etc/shadow` file in hash format.

124. A. The traffic of the data is annotated by the ->, which is the direction in which the file is being downloaded. The socket address is 172.16.1.100:56209.

125. B. The user ray is a valid user account. You can determine the user in in the `/etc/shadow` if there is hash value associated with the subject's account. In this case, our hash begins with 6xHEKhMr2.

Chapter 3: Practice Test 3

1. D. The Simple Network Management Protocol is a protocol that is used with network appliances and nodes. You can gather statistical, performance, and status updates from your devices with this protocol. SSH is Secure Shell, NTP is the Network Time Protocol, and SMNP is just SNMP with the order of the letters mangled.

2. B. An extranet is a subnet that functions like a DMZ, but it allows two businesses that depend on one another to share resources.

3. D. A Class C subnet has 256 bits. Subtracting 192 bits from 256 bits results in 64 hosts per subnet. Dividing 256 by 64 provides 4 usable networks.

4. B. The file location is `/etc/shadow`, and it contains a list of passwords that are hashed. In most cases, this file is hidden if you are not in the root account. The `/etc/passwd` file is where user information is stored, but it does not include password hashes or any other password information.

5. D. When you enter the command su root, you are prompted with the root password. If it's entered correctly, you can switch from your profile to the root account and have administrator-level privileges on the operating system. su is short for switch user. The sudo command is a way to temporarily assume another user's privileges for the purpose of executing a single command. Typically, this would be done to elevate privileges to root level. By contrast, when you execute su, you maintain the permissions of the new user until you execute the shell of that user.

6. B. TLS uses RSA 1024 or the 2048-bit key strength during key negotiation. In most web browsers, you are able to view this information in the Security tab in the preferences panel. AES may be used during the session for encryption but would not be used for key negotiation. ECE isn't anything, and PGP is not used for TLS.

7. A. A baseline must be set in order for an anomaly detection system to run optimally. If not, the IDS will not be able to monitor network traffic accurately and may alert due to false positives. Anomaly-based IDS does not use definitions or signatures. Neither network infrastructure nor client updates will help with getting an anomaly-based IDS working, aside from just being a good idea generally.

8. D. The MX, or mail exchange, record is the record that is used in a DNS server to identify the actual mail server. The SOA record is the start of authority record and is used to provide information about the domain itself. An A record is an IPv4 address, used to map a hostname with an IP address. A CNAME is a canonical name, or an alias, allowing a hostname to be mapped to another hostname, which may have an IP address associated with it.

9. C. While you could use DNS poisoning, a better approach would be to use ARP spoofing, where you tell every system on the network your MAC address maps to all of the IP addresses. DNS spoofing would require either ARP spoofing to intercept all the DNS requests or the compromise of a local caching DNS server to catch all requests. Additionally, DNS spoofing only gets you traffic where a hostname has to be resolved. ARP spoofing gets all IP traffic. Phishing is used to socially engineer a user and packet fragmentation may be used to evade detection.

10. A. Older intrusion detection systems may have had a harder time reconstructing packets that had been fragmented. With extreme fragmentation, it may have been harder for these systems to reconstruct and identify issues fast enough. Extreme fragmentation or delays may allow bad packets to get through because the intrusion detection system doesn't want to hold anything up while it waits to reconstruct a packet. Newer systems would be better able to keep up. Additionally, they would know this is an evasion technique. ARP spoofing and DNS hijacking are not used for evasion. Phishing is not a technique used to get traffic into a network.

11. A. Attackers are moving to using tools available on Windows systems, just as they have used existing scripting languages on Unix-like systems. PowerShell is a powerful tool that has existed on every Windows system for several versions. When attackers use existing system tools, it's called living off the land. PowerShell is not supposed to be encrypted or obfuscated in normal usage. Updating PowerShell does not explain the obfuscated script.

12. A. HKEY_LOCAL_MACHINE\SAM is the Registry entry where the SAM and SAM.log parameters can be found.

13. C. When scanning for SNMP using Metasploit, the command is `use auxiliary/scanner/snmp/<device name>`. Once that is set, you will set your listening and receiving host information and then execute the scan by entering `run` into the command line.

14. B. In the command line, when searching for a particular string, you use the `grep` command to search for contents. Most often, administrators would pipe the string into another command or to an output format such as a text document. The command `ls` is used to list files. The `info` utility is an alternative to the man pages on a Linux system.

15. D. When you're using `msfencode` in Metasploit, the payload will be converted into a raw output format. Encoding the payload allows the signature of your malware to be changed, greatly decreasing your ability to be detected by signature-based technologies.

16. A. Malware often communicates with a command-and-control infrastructure (C2) infrastructure managed by the attacker. This may be another compromised system. *Command processor* may be another term for a program allowing command-line access. The other answers are not correct.

17. B. Buffers provide static data storage capacity. When data is allocated to that storage and is found to be too large, it causes a buffer overflow in which arbitrary commands can be executed or data can be overwritten. Dynamic data storage is kept on the heap and isn't commonly called a buffer. A buffer isn't data in transit, though a buffer may be used on either end of the conversation.

18. A. The variable `attacker` is used to store a character string that is 5 bytes long. The first `strcpy` will overflow that buffer, but it may cause no problem aside from potentially crashing the program. The `scanf()` call may cause an attacker to be able to control the flow of execution. While there is a command in the `strcpy()` call, this is not a command injection because nothing is done with the command that is copied into the variable, especially since the command is too long to be stored in the buffer. Heap spraying requires dynamically allocated memory. SQL injection is done in a web application.

19. B. Boundary checking is validating all input. If a user inputs a value that is greater than the memory allocated for it, the program will return with an invalid operation. It will continue to do so until the user inputs a value that is within the specified container value.

20. C. It is highly recommended to initialize variables with a value that is pertinent to its function. If you don't initialize the variable, data residue may still be present, and when it comes time to execute a set of instructions, the data output may not be accurate.

21. D. Heaps are used during the execution of a program. Because a program can have dynamic processes, heaps are used to allocate the amount of memory for it. Registers are memory that is stored in the CPU. Swapfiles are where data is stored that is swapped out of memory. Static allocation of memory is done on the stack.

22. B. Programs that are initially executed have a segment in memory allocated called a stack. A stack has a fixed allocation of memory when it is created. The heap is where dynamic memory is allocated. A pointer is a variable that points at a memory location. A cluster doesn't mean anything in this context but could mean different things, which means more context is needed.

23. **A.** DNS requests are commonly sent to a local caching server, which looks in its cache. A failure there causes a request to root servers and then subsequent servers, always getting closer to the final destination. This process of asking a question, getting an answer, and asking again using the new information is called *recursion*. Neither iterative nor combinatorics make sense in this context, and bistromathics is a field of study invented by Douglas Adams for the book *Life, the Universe and Everything*.

24. **D.** MegaPing can be used for scanning networks, nbtstat is used to gather information about NetBIOS on Windows systems, and dig is used to collect information from DNS servers. theHarvester is used to collect information like email addresses from PGP servers, Bing, Google and LinkedIn.

25. **A.** The tool packETH can be used to craft packets with data in both the headers and payload that is set to what you want it to be set to. You wouldn't use packETH for any of the other purposes.

26. **A.** The adversary must first track the session before making a successful attempt at hijacking it. Desynchronizing isn't a thing, and the other techniques would come after tracking the session.

27. **A.** ISO 27001 is a standard for managing information security, including a set of controls and how to manage those controls. This includes the cycle Plan, Do, Check, Act. ISO 27002 (formerly 17799) is the standard that lays out guidelines for information system security managers who initiate, put into action, and maintain information security within an organization. NIST 800-53 is a set of controls managed by the National Institute of Standards and Technology. NIST 800-161 is a document related to supply chain management.

28. **C.** Key loggers come in hardware and software packages. They are used to covertly capture the victim's key strokes at a terminal to be later retrieved by the adversary to replay their credentials. While a key logger may be malware, there are a lot of other types of malware. Spyware is used to monitor activity on a system without necessarily logging key strokes. Recordware is not a thing.

29. **C.** Community strings contain data that provides authentication. Depending on the type of string, it will provide the user with a certain level of privileges. For example, the public community string derives only a read-only privilege. None of the other answers is used within SNMP.

30. **C.** A canonical name (CNAME) record provides an alias to a domain name. This maps a hostname to another hostname. While you may have multiple aliases, at some point there needs to be an A record to map a hostname to an IP address. While an alias to an alias is considered a bad idea because of efficiency, there is nothing that specifically prohibits it, which means you can end up with a set of aliases that never resolve to an address and that's allowed by the standard.

31. **A.** Adware is a type of malware that creates pop-up windows on the desktop to advertise for commercial products. *Malware* is a generic term that encompasses multiple types of malicious software. Pop-up blockers are used in browsers to prevent sites from opening up a new window. Freeware is a type of software that doesn't cost money.

32. **B.** Availability ensures that data is readily available to the customer. Redundancy may be used to ensure availability. CIA is often referred to as the triad in this context (as separate from the Central Intelligence Agency) and refers to confidentiality, integrity, and availability. Survivability doesn't mean anything in this context.

33. D. A proxy server is a device that acts as a buffer between user workstations, which are trusted, and servers commonly outside the enterprise, which are untrusted. Connections originated from the user system will pass through the proxy, which will originate the message to the server. A firewall doesn't sit in the middle of the conversation like this. A proxy can be a gateway of sorts, but there are different types of gateways, and a gateway doesn't necessarily participate in the conversation in the same way a proxy server does.

34. C. RMI is a way to implement interprocess communications using Java. Since Java is an object-oriented programming language, it would transmit objects. SMB is the Server Message Block protocol. Portmapper is a program that is used for remote procedure calls.

35. A. LOIC, or Low Orbit Ion Cannon, is an application that can be used to conduct a DDoS on a system by using TCP, UDP, or HTTP requests. Cain & Abel is used for cracking passwords. The other two are not real answers.

36. D. The UPDATE command is used to update data in a record in a table. Depending on the situation, the adversary can add, create, or even change an administrator's password in a SQL database. DROP is a SQL statement used to remove a table or database from the database system. ADD may be used to add columns. COPY is used to copy data between entities.

37. C. A deauthentication attack sends a deauthentication message to the station, causing it to send a new authentication message. This will allow the attacker to collect this authentication information for cracking later. A rogue access point may collect authentication information, but it wouldn't force reauthentication. Neither WEP cracking nor a handshaking attack is relevant here.

38. B. John the Ripper is a program that allows an individual to crack an account. LOIC is the Low Orbit Ion Cannon application, used to cause a denial of service on web servers. Wireshark is a packet capture program. CPU Dump is not the name of a real program.

39. B. The Internet segment is the third layer in the TCP/IP model, which is equivalent to the Network layer in the OSI model. There is no Network layer in the TCP/IP architecture. The Transport layer in the TCP/IP architecture maps to the Transport layer in the OSI model.

40. B. The FIN flag set informs the distant end to terminate its connection with the sender. No action will be taken after it is set. The SYN flag is used to initiate a connection. The PSH flag is used to get data sent immediately to the application rather than being held in a buffer. The RST flag is used to reset a connection.

41. A. Angry IP is an application that provides an array of tools for ping sweeping. Depending on the configuration, there is a good chance an IPS/IDS appliance will detect your presence conducting ping sweeps. Cain & Abel is used to crack passwords. Nmap can be used to perform ping sweeps, but the parameters provided would be used to perform a very slow full connect TCP scan. nslookup is used to perform DNS lookups.

42. A. Cain & Abel is an application that provides an array of tools to the user, such as tools for password cracking, ARP spoofing, and conducting man-in-the-middle attacks. Evercrack is a way some people refer to the game *Everquest*. Kismet is used for wireless sniffing, and John the Ripper is a password cracking tool.

43. B. A cross-site scripting attack targets the client side since the script runs in the user's browser. XML external entity injection, SQL injection, and command injection all target the server since all injected code runs on the server, either in the OS or the database server.

44. B. Identity theft is the process in which the adversary impersonates the victim in order to gain some type of access to the victim's financial resources or other critical resources.

45. A. BackTrack used to be the primary distribution for a hacker or pen tester to use. Since then, it has been replaced with Kali Linux. Security Onion is most associated with defender or detection toolkits. Ubuntu and Mint are both regular desktop-oriented Linux distributions.

46. D. Brazil is in South America, which is considered to be in Latin America. This means it falls under the Latin America and Caribbean Network Information Center. AFRINIC covers Africa. RIPE covers Europe, and APNIC is the Asia Pacific Network Information Center.

47. B. NIST, or National Institute of Standards and Technology, is a government organization that provides standards to an array of industries, including standards for information systems management and cryptology. EC-Council manages the Certified Ethical Hacker certification. CAIN and NITS aren't anything in this context.

48. D. The interface to the backend of a mobile application is likely to be a RESTful API. Behind the API, you may find a NoSQL database or microservices, though the first point of contact will be the API.

49. A. The first server you are likely to pass through is the web server. You would be looking to get to the application server, but the first server would be the web server. The database server would only be reached after passing through the web server and the application server. There is no logic server, though business logic is what would be implemented in the application server.

50. C. Clark-Wilson uses unconstrained data items (UDIs) and constrained data items (CDIs) to talk about the integrity of data objects. The other answers here don't make sense in this context. UTC, for example, is Coordinated Universal Time.

51. C. When clients communicate directly with one another without the aid of a wireless access point, they are communicating in ad hoc mode. Clients don't have to connect through a wireless access point (WAP). The other answers don't make sense in this context.

52. D. Monitor mode allows the wireless adapter to receive the packets, read them, and then forward them to the sniffer. This allows traffic at the radio layer to be captured. While promiscuous mode is used to capture network traffic usually, it is not enough to capture wireless traffic, meaning down to layer 2.

53. A. With a phone call, you can have a conversation with the victim and go into more detail. Not everyone has a phone, just as not everyone has email. Phishing attacks are often successful. Pretexting does not require the use of a phone.

54. C. The iris is the pattern in the area around the pupil. This is the colored part of the eye, and it has a distinct pattern, which is different from everyone else. The retina is a layer at the back of the eye, which is also distinct. Fingerprint scanning is also unique but not related to the eye. The uvea is part of the eye but is not used to identify individuals.

55. B. A false failure rate, also called a false reject rate, is an indication of the number of legitimate users whose authentication attempts result in failure. This means, in the case of building entry, a number of people are not being allowed access. This would not result in people needing to change passwords and may not have anything to do with a mantrap. While it may result in the biometric system being investigated, it won't result in people not using biometrics, especially if that's the way the company has decided to authenticate individuals.

56. B. HTTP is a stateless protocol, which requires the application to perform some sort of state transfer. REST is representational state transfer, which allows the client and server to communicate information about the state of the client and the application between them. HTML is not a protocol but a language, so state doesn't make sense.

57. D. The Transmission Control Protocol follows a three-step handshake, which is really four steps, but two are collapsed into a single step. For each side of the conversation, a SYN message needs to be sent to indicate the starting sequence number. The other side needs to acknowledge receipt of that value. Therefore, the client sends out a SYN. The server replies by acknowledging the client's SYN while simultaneously sending a SYN of its own. The client then responds with an ACK. This means the sequence is SYN, SYN/ACK, ACK. FIN is used to tear down the connection when communication is at an end.

58. B. Each full octet is 8 bits, which means 255.255.255.0 is 3 bytes of 8 bits, or a total of 24 bits. With CIDR, we count the number of bits in the subnet mask. Since 255.255.255.0 is 24 bits, 255.255.254.0 is one less bit. The last bit would make the value of that third octet 255. That means instead of /24, we have a CIDR designation of /23.

59. A. Port 53 is used to conduct DNS resolutions and zone transfers. Ports 80 and 8080 are used for HTTP communication. Port 25 is used for email using SMTP.

60. A. Bluejacking is the technique used by attackers to send data to a device without going through the pairing typically necessary for Bluetooth devices. Blueboxing isn't really a thing, though blue boxes were used to make free phone calls decades ago. Bluesnarfing is grabbing data from a Bluetooth device, and Bluebugging is using a Bluetooth device to listen in on someone.

61. C. UDP does not use any flags. TCP uses both RST and FIN. UDP is a connectionless protocol, so there is no need to terminate any connection.

62. D. Traceroute is a useful tool because it will tell the administrator what path the packets are taking and possibly inform the administrator of firewalls within its path.

63. A. TTL is a header that defines the lifetime of a packet on the network. A value such as 64 is assigned, and every time the packet reaches a layer 3 device (router), the value decrements by 1. When it reaches zero, the router will drop the packet and send back an ICMP error message indicating the time was exceeded in transit.

64. B. An NS record indicates the name server associated with a domain. This may include subdomains, which is why sometimes the term *zone* is used since *domain* can be ambiguous. Domains and subdomains each have their own zone and require an NS record to indicate the name server used for that zone. A PTR record is used to provide a hostname mapping to an IP address. None of the other answers is relevant to DNS.

65. B. The -sI switch allows the user to conduct an idle scan. It is used to gather the IP address of the target system by crafting special packets that are bounced off a zombie machine.

66. D. While Nmap is an excellent program in its own right and can be used to enumerate data across multiple services, it doesn't store data in a database for retrieval later without some additional help. Metasploit can also be used to enumerate data across multiple services and also uses a database on the back end to store data to be retrieved later. Nessus is used to scan for vulnerabilities, and Masscan can be used to perform rapid port scans on large networks.

67. B. The layers of the OSI model from the bottom are Physical, Data Link, Network, Transport, Session, Presentation, and Application. This makes the Network layer number 3.

68. B. While flooding a switch can sometimes work to get the switch to send all frames to every port, it's not guaranteed, and the effect is not the same as ARP spoofing anyway. Sending gratuitous ARP responses mapping an IP address to an attacker's ARP address can get frames sent to the attacker. There isn't any such thing as a gratuitous ARP request since a request is a request for information. A gratuitous response is a response in the absence of a request.

69. C. A pre-shared key is one that has to be known ahead of time in order to encrypt data. Asymmetric and symmetric encryption are types of encryption, not keys. You can have a secret key that isn't known ahead of time since keys can be mutually derived at the time they are needed.

70. A. Cross-site scripting would include a <SCRIPT> tag in some fashion. Cross-site request forgery would just be a link to a third-party site. What you are seeing is an XML tag that calls out to a system function. While command injection would call system functions, it does not use XML to send the message.

71. D. arpspoof is a tool that will allow the ability to temporarily spoof the MAC address on a network interface card. None of the other answers is a real tool.

72. D. Phone calls for social engineering are not guaranteed for success any more than email is. You can go into detail with a phishing message. Pretexting is something that is done no matter the medium for the social engineering attack. You may get access to more people with the phone than with email, and the people you access may be less sophisticated in recognizing these types of attacks.

73. B. SNMPv3 (Simple Network Management Protocol version 3) is the most recent version of SNMP for network device management. It adds encryption and user authentication in order to allow management messaging and polling to be sent to devices. ICMP is the Internet Control Message Protocol, which is used to send control and error messages across the Internet. It does not require authentication. IMAP is used to retrieve email messages, and there are older versions of SNMP that do not allow for encryption or authentication.

74. D. An evil twin is wireless access point that is made to look like an actual legitimate WAP. The adversary is tempting users to reconnect to it by having the victims send their credentials. The adversary hopes to gain financial information when the victims conduct e-commerce transactions. A rogue AP is just an access point on an enterprise network that has not been authorized. These were common when businesses were just starting to embrace wireless for people who wanted to be able to use mobile devices and connect to the enterprise network.

75. A. The Iran nuclear centrifuges were infected with the Stuxnet viruses. It caused the centrifuges to spin out of control, causing irrecoverable physical damage. ILOVEYOU was an email-based worm, and BackOrifice is a remote access tool that was often installed as a Trojan.

76. D. EXPN is used to expand mailing lists. EHLO is how you would greet an extended SMTP server. VRML is not a command used for SMTP. You may be able to use VRFY (verify) to check an email address.

77. C. A SQL injection attack sends Structured Query Language code into the web application. This is a language that runs in relational database servers to perform functions on the data stored there. It may pass through a web server and an application server, but it executes on a database server.

78. B. POODLE, which stands for Padding Oracle On Downgraded Legacy Encryption, exploits the SSL 3.0 requests. After the last request, the attacker will be able to retrieve 1 byte of data that is between the client and server.

79. B. Tor is a network comprising volunteered private routers that build a network based on confidentially and is free to use. Tor was developed in the mid-1990s by the United States Naval Research Laboratory. Tor is an initialism meaning The Onion Router.

80. C. A ticket-granting service provides access to a subject for a certain resource or object.

81. A. A signature-based IDS must have an up-to-date signature list, which are a set of rules used to accurately alert and defend against attacks.

82. D. A Smurf attack is one where ICMP messages are used to get large volumes of responses sent to a target. Similarly, a Fraggle attack uses UDP messages to cause the same effect. As the goal is to get large volumes of messages sent to a victim, this is an amplification attack.

83. D. Bodo Moller, Thai Duong, and Krysztof Kotowicz published the vulnerability to the public domain on October 14, 2014.

84. C. There are four fields in a UDP header: source and destination port as well as checksum and length.

85. C. An executive summary is a high-level view of the overall penetration testing results. It is geared toward senior officials and managers.

86. D. Separation of duties is the principle that requires two or more people to perform a task. These tasks are usually tied to a sensitive action such as making a large deposit in a bank or even launching nuclear weapons from a submarine. It prevents one person or entity from having complete unadulterated control over a task or function.

87. C. Google Hacking uses sets of keywords to be able to narrow the results provided by Google. While this may be used for reconnaissance, it's used for other purposes as well. In addition, reconnaissance can be performed many other ways. The `filename:` keyword suggests you are looking for documents, but this is not called doxing. You would not use this keyword for IoT device lookups.

88. B. Nmap does support port scanning. Both Nmap and Metasploit support scripting interfaces. Metasploit is unlikely to be any faster when it does port scans. It does, though, store results in a database so the results can be looked up later.

89. D. Availability is part of the triad that deals with how easy or difficult it is to use resources or data. The easier it is to access data, the less secure it may be, but it's also true that the harder it is to access, the less likely it will be compromised and the more likely work production will be slowed down.

90. C. Even though using a shredder is a physical control to prevent information from being leaked, a mandatory policy was used to get the organization to conform.

91. B. Port address translation (PAT) uses the source computer's port number as a unique web session when the packet leaves the local network.

92. A. The macro feature that was once enabled by default when you installed Microsoft Office is now disabled. The ILOVEYOU virus took advantage of that capability by capturing contacts in users' email address books and sending out mass copies of itself to those recipients.

93. C. AES is the Advanced Encryption Standard. It is used to encrypt messages. It may be used with a message authentication code but wouldn't generate one. PGP is used for key management. Other encryption algorithms may be used for the actual encryption of messages using PGP. MB4 does not exist. SHA is the secure hash algorithm, which could be used to generate a cryptographic hash that is used for message authentication codes.

94. B. In Linux, the / set by itself denotes that the user is currently residing in the root directory. None of the other answers indicates a specific directory in Linux.

95. A. Role-based access control, or RBAC, is an access control model that is developed around a job position. For example, if you worked at a bank as a teller, your login resources are tailored to what a bank teller would have access to. It is a cookie-cutter type of profile that aids in controlling employee access and limits capabilities to do one and only one job.

96. D. Passive reconnaissance is the act of gathering as much knowledge and intelligence you can without directly impacting operations of the target. Although it is much harder to gather information through this phase, it almost guarantees that as a black hat, you and your operation will not be compromised.

97. C. The rule header defines the rule type, the protocol, the source IP and port, the direction, and then the destination IP address and the port.

98. A. Time to live (TTL) is a value set on IP packets that decrements each and every time they pass through a router. Some operating systems, such as Linux and Microsoft, will set the TTL value. When the TTL value of a packet reaches 0, that packet will be dropped, and an ICMP destination not found message will be returned to the source.

99. B. When the security administrators are no longer following the security policies set in place by the organization, it is a telltale sign that the policies are not up-to-date. Policies should be evaluated often because the operational tempo and working environment can be and will be dynamic.

100. C. Session splicing is the process of breaking up a payload among different packets that the IDS may ignore. When the host receives all of the packets and processes them, the exploit may trigger the arbitrary payload the adversary has sent, such as installing malware or providing a reverse command shell.

101. A. If a switch receives too many sets of instructions and it cannot keep up with the demand, it fails open. Fail open is when the switch does not separate traffic anymore by collision domains and thus will flood out all the traffic to all of the ports, much like a hub. If the adversary can do this, they can now receive all the traffic that is broadcast from all of the computers connected to the switch.

102. D. The -sS conducts a SYN scan, and the -O scans the system and fingerprints for an operating system type.

103. B. SSID scanning would be used to identify available wireless networks. A deauthentication attack might be used to gather data that could be used in an encryption attack. Injections are used for deauthentication attacks. An evil twin is a rogue access point masquerading as a legitimate access point in order to gather authentication data.

104. C. Probing the firewall with ACK flagged messages will determine what firewall rules may be in place.

105. C. Once a SYN message has been sent, the communication is considered to be NEW. If the traffic is a different stream that has an association with an existing stream, it would be considered RELATED. There is no STATELESS state. Once the three-way handshake has been completed, the communication is considered to be ESTABLISHED.

106. B. TamperData can be used to alter data between the browser and the server (and vice versa). GreaseMonkey allows user scripts to be run. Nova isn't something that makes sense in this context. WappAlyzer is a plugin that determines the technologies in use on a website.

107. B. The Internet Security Association and Key Management Protocol (ISAKMP) is responsible for negotiating and conducting the key agreement.

108. D. ICMP Type 11 provides the source with a "Time Exceeded" response. Time exceeded is more prevalent if satellite communications are involved and an IP booster is not in use.

109. D. The Lightweight Extensible Authentication Protocol (LEAP) is a Cisco proprietary protocol and can be used in place of TKIP.

110. A. NBT (NetBIOS over TCP/IP) uses UDP 137; NetBIOS session uses TCP 139; NetBIOS datagram uses UDP 138.

111. A. While Twitter and Facebook will sometimes have details that could be useful, LinkedIn contains a lot of information about companies, employees, and technology that may be in use. Friendster is a defunct social networking site, and WhatsApp is a direct messaging platform.

112. A. The WAP will send out a beacon frame advertising its SSID to wireless devices. A broadcast frame is used to send a layer 2 message to every device in a broadcast or collision domain. Neither of the other two answers is real in this context.

113. C. Implementing user and security awareness training is a cost-effective solution. Not only does it raise awareness in the organization, it is also free to implement.

114. A. Stateful firewall keeps track of all communications and inspects the packets. This can help protect against things like spoofed packets, where a state is trying to be faked with headers. Although this capability does slow down the network, it provides an extra layer of defense.

115. B. In this scenario, you are conducting gray box testing. Because you are given a network mask to go off on, you now know how big of a network you are testing. Even though this is your only clue, it is still partial knowledge of the environment that you are now operating in.

116. A. AES is an encryption algorithm. Encryption addresses the need for confidentiality. While some elements of the encryption process can protect integrity, encryption primarily addresses confidentiality.

117. B. In a hybrid-mesh topology, a mesh topology is participating in another topology.

118. A. A dual-homed firewall is one that has two network interface cards (NICs). The more NICs you have, the more you can segment networks with. In this case, the firewall is managing two different subnets based on the logical diagram.

119. D. The flags portion is missing. The URG, ACK, PSH, RST, SYN, and FIN flags are used in TCP connections.

120. D. Sequence numbers are incremented each time the source sends a packet to the destination. The acknowledgment value is what the receiver can expect next from the sender. To determine the total sequence amount, if the ACK is set to 200 (or whatever value it is determined to be at the time) and a window size is set to 170, the client can expect sequence numbers from 200 to 370. To complete the TCP connection, the final flag is set to ACK.

121. C. A rootkit is a set of tools or applications that can have direct administrator and kernel access to a computer. This poses a significant problem because it is very hard to detect because the kernel or root level is the most secured part of the operating system.

122. C. BlueBug is a way of gaining access to a Bluetooth device and getting it to place a phone call. Once the call has been completed, the called party can listen in on anything happening in the vicinity of the phone. The other answers don't exist.

123. A. In a Smurf attack, the adversary spoofs a victim's IP address and then pings the broadcast address. All nodes on that network segment will send back an ICMP echo reply, causing a DoS on the victim's system.

124. B. Shoulder surfing is a passive attack. Simply peering over the shoulder of an unsuspecting person is one of the easiest ways to capture credentials with.

125. D. Whenever a client is trying to establish a Secure Sockets Layer connection, the first packet is flagged to "Don't Fragment." This prevents an adversary from injecting their own packets in the middle of a secure data stream.

Chapter 4: Practice Test 4

1.   A. RSA uses two prime numbers that are factored together and can create a key size up to 4,096 bits. The RSA algorithm can be used for digital signatures and encryption. This is typically done with asymmetric encryption algorithms. Symmetric encryption ciphers like AES, for instance, use a different technique.

2.   B. In asymmetric encryption, two keys known as the public and private key are mathematically related. Asymmetric encryption uses two separate keys; one of them is for encrypting, and the other is for decrypting.

3.   D. Transport mode provides protection to the payload through encryption. Transport mode leaves the original headers intact, meaning only the payload is protected. Tunnel mode provides encryption to protect the message header and the payload. A separate message header is placed on messages using tunnel mode. Otherwise, the intermediate devices would not be able to read the source and destination addresses. The new source address would be whatever device was meant to be the recipient of the IPSec message. This may not necessarily be the endpoint sending the message, since there may be a network device that takes care of handling the encryption and transit from one network to another.

4.   B. Request for Comments (RFC) 1918 defines 10.0.0.0–10.255.255.255, 172.16.0.0–172.31.255.255, and 192.168.0.0–192.168.255.255 as private, non-routable IP addresses.

5.   B. An A record maps an IPv4 address to a hostname. It is the most commonly used DNS record type. A user can alter the host file by inputting an IP address followed by a domain name or hostname. An MX record is an mail exchanger record, indicating a mail server. There are no AAA records, though an AAAA record refers to an IPv6 address. There is no MR record.

6.   C. A kerberoasting attack abuses the Kerberos protocol that is used to authenticate users to systems and services on a Windows-based network. EternalBlue is an exploit against the Server Message Block protocol used on Windows systems. A Smurf attack uses ICMP messages to perform a denial-of-service attack. Rainbow tables are used to quickly crack passwords.

7.   B. URL obfuscation is the process of changing a value so it means the same but is in a different format. For example, instead of using `http://22.56.98.4`, you would convert the IP address to binary, which is 00010110001110000110001000000100. Then to ensure that the value will work properly with the browser, you convert the binary value into decimal format, which is `http://372793860`. This may allow you to bypass firewall restrictions since a binary rule may not be configured for the firewall.

8.   A. Social engineering encompasses all the options. It is the process of tricking and manipulating people into, for example, opening spam email, providing account login information over the phone, or allowing the attacker to piggyback or tailgate through a physical security device. Training employees on social engineering is a cost-effective solution for preventing such incidents.

9. C. An evil twin attack mimics an existing access point by using the same SSID. This might get victims to connect to your access point, providing authentication credentials. BlueSnarf is a Bluetooth attack. A rogue access point is one that is not authorized to be attached to the enterprise network and may not be used to gather passwords but just to provide convenient wireless access to users. KRAKEN is not an attack that relates to wireless networking.

10. D. RC4 in WEP uses anywhere from 40- to 232-bit keys for encryption. The weakness in WEP is not the encryption itself but rather the initialization vector, which is the seed value from which to begin encryption. If the adversary can gather enough packets, they can derive the key used for encryption.

11. B. MSConfig provides the user with different applications affiliated with Startup, Services, and Boot. Among other things, MSConfig can inform the user what applications currently in startup may have been remotely or covertly installed. Regedit can be used to look at Registry entries, which would include the locations where services may be installed and other pro-grams could be set to autorun. However, Regedit won't show you anything on the file system.

12. C. There are four stages in the handshake between a station and an access point. This is done to perform mutual authentication to ensure both ends of the communication are valid and allowed.

13. A. The * symbol is a value that means *everything*. The statement SELECT * FROM Vegetables queries a SQL database to "select everything from the Vegetables table." The request being sent to the SQL database will then return all the values listed in the Vegetables table.

14. B. hping3 can be used to perform port scans and other types of attack based on sending crafted packets to servers on specific ports. The others could be used to brute-force direc-tories and page names to identify objects that might be accessible directly.

15. C. The ticket-granting ticket (TGT) is provided to the key distribution center (KDC). If the ticket is legitimate, the KDC will issue a ticket-granting service (TGS) ticket. The subject will then present the ticket-granting service ticket to the server and will be provided with access to the system or resource that was originally requested.

16. D. When you want to use a compromised system effectively as a router, you are using a tech-nique called pivoting. Privilege escalation is also a post-exploitation technique used to gain additional permissions on a system. Kerberoasting is collecting password information from Kerberos messages. Trampolining is not a thing in this context.

17. B. You would send messages that deauthenticate a station from an access point. This forces the station to reauthenticate so you can collect the authentication messages, which might allow you to crack the credentials. An evil twin is also used to gather credentials but it's done by pretending to be a legitimate access point. KRACK is a key reinstallation attack. A rogue AP is an illegitimate access point connected to a business network.

18. A. UDP is a simple protocol. There is just a source and destination port for headers. This means there are no other header fields to determine or control a connection between one endpoint and another. There are not other techniques as is the case with TCP, which uses flags and also is connection-oriented.

19. A. The short message service (SMS) is used to send text messages. This means you are using smishing to send a phishing message over SMS. Vishing is voice phishing. Whaling is phishing against high-value targets.

20. D. The tool nbtstat is built into Windows systems to collect information about the NetBIOS network. NetBIOS is an older set of services used to interact with Windows-based networks. In order to collect information about these networks, you can use nbtstat. The tool ipconfig is used to get IP configuration on Windows systems. MSConfig is a program showing system information on Windows systems. Netstat is used to get network information like listening ports.

21. B. Social engineering is used to get users to perform acts they otherwise wouldn't perform. *Spam* is another word for unsolicited commercial email. If you were gathering credentials, you wouldn't send commercial emails. Whaling is phishing against high-value targets. Neither of these techniques would be done by calling a target. *Manipulation* is too general a term for this question.

22. A. Operational technology is used for process automation, which might include programmable logic controllers to interact with devices. This could include being an interface to collect operational data like flow rates in water processing plants, for instance. None of the other answers is an example of operational technology.

23. B. Fuzzing is a technique that inserts random input values into a system. The purpose of fuzzing is to determine how a program or an application may respond to certain types of input. This can aid in troubleshooting when applications are developed or penetration testing operations are conducted.

24. D. A quick and easy way to get to a mobile device is with a smishing attack, where a text message is sent to a mobile device with a malicious URL. If the recipient visits the URL and it has appropriate code, it could be used to compromise the device. Buffer overflow is not an easy thing to accomplish, especially given the languages in which mobile apps may be written. SQL injection would not work on a mobile device and a remote screen lock wouldn't accomplish what you want.

25. B. The client has been authenticated once it receives its ticket-granting ticket (TGT) and is then considered an authenticated principal in the Kerberos realm. Although the client received the TGT, that does not necessarily mean they have access to all of the resources.

26. C. By targeting the HVAC units, the black hat has the potential to DoS all the systems in the server room. The heat must be raised to a high enough temperature to cause the peripherals to overheat and crash. The heat generated by the servers along with the HVAC temperature being raised will ensure a quick DoS state and minimize the response time of the security administrators. Targeting the routers would impact the routers. Changing the administrator login information, were it possible, would lock out administrators but not prevent users from getting to services.

27. C. Searchsploit is a tool that is available on Linux systems like Kali Linux and Parrot OS. It searches through the Exploit-DB repository of exploits for proof of concept or other exploit code. Zed Attack Proxy is used for web application testing. Nessus is used to look for vulnerabilities on systems. EDGAR contains financial records from publicly traded companies.

28. A. The tool msfvenom can be used to easily package up any module in Metasploit into an executable. This could be used to deploy to a victim system to connect back to listening infrastructure, which might also be managed by Metasploit. hping3 is a packet crafting and scanning tool. OpenVAS is used to scan for vulnerabilities, and ven0m0us does not exist.

29. C. Shodan was designed as a search engine for Internet of Things–related devices like web-cams. Additionally, operational technology devices can be found using Shodan. This includes industrial control systems. Shodan could also be used to find default passwords in the devices in their database. It cannot be used to identify IP address ranges for a company.

30. B. The Caesar cipher uses two alphabets: one with the plain text, while the second one is rotated some number of characters. Rot13 uses the Caesar cipher. Rijndael is the name of the Advanced Encryption Standard cipher. Vignere uses a matrix of two alphabets: one across the top, with another down the side. You use the intersection of the rows and columns to encrypt/decrypt based on where you are in the message.

31. C. Dividing large networks by creating VLANS and subnets makes them more manageable, which may include implementing controls that are specific to the systems on one network segment that wouldn't be necessary for the systems on another one.

32. B. In a Platform as a Service implementation, the provider would have responsibility for the operating system as well as the application server. The client would be responsible for the code they develop and run in the platform (application server).

33. D. While all of these are potentially bad, weak access management is a common vulnerability in cloud computing deployments. Poor protections on credentials continues to be a problem in the information technology space, regardless of where the systems are deployed.

34. A. Top Secret is the highest classification used. To be granted this security label, you have to meet a need-to-know requirement.

35. B. A buffer overflow attack is used to manipulate the flow of execution of a program and is achieved by sending more data into a program than is allocated in memory. Cross-site script-ing would use a scripting language, and command injection would mean you'd see operating system commands. Heap spraying is also used to manipulate the flow of execution but does not use more data than has been allocated to work.

36. C. The PTR, or pointer, record type is used to map an IP address to a hostname. Mapping a hostname to an IP address uses an A record. The MX record indicates the mail exchanger system for the domain, and the NS record indicates the name server.

37. D. Polymorphism is where malware takes a different form for every system it runs on. The exe-cutable would have different markers, like a cryptographic hash, making it hard for anti-malware software to detect it. While encryption and packing (*compression* is another word for packing) may be used, unless the file signature changes, these can be detected once they are known.

38. D. A unified threat management device may be able to detect malware in the network as it combines a number of traditional technologies, including a firewall but also intrusion detec-tion. Antivirus and endpoint detection and response software runs on the endpoint, not in the network. A stateful firewall would not be able to detect malicious software.

39. B. Exploit-DB is an online database of information, including source code, that may include either proofs of concept or actual exploits against known vulnerabilities. LinkedIn is helpful for reconnaissance but would not include exploit code. The same is true for Twitter. There is no Metasploit-DB site online.

40. D. The utility mimikatz is often used by attackers to extract passwords from memory and from the system Registry. This program is available as stand-alone as well as in Metasploit as a loadable module in a Meterpreter session. Nmap is used for port scanning, and lsass is the Local Security Authority Subsystem Service and is used for authentication on Windows systems. CryptCat can be used to initiate and receive encrypted network communications.

41. B. Getting an app into the App Store may be the most effective, though this can be challenging if the App Store in question is performing strong application vetting. Port scanning won't compromise a system, and neither password compromise nor phishing alone will get you a compromise of a mobile device.

42. C. The original sender receives a SYN/ACK from the receiver signifying the acknowledgment of the SYN packet.

43. A. In cloud-native designs, developers are often using databases built on NoSQL. This means SQL injection won't work since there is nothing that can run SQL queries on the back end. Cross-site scripting and cross-site request forgery are targeted at the user end of the application, so they would be successful as much with cloud-native as anything else. XML external entity is still valid since these applications still use XML to communicate between client and server.

44. B. When the RST flag is set, it forces the sender to close their connection as well alerting the receiver on the network to close their connection as well. A FIN message can be used to terminate an open connection but wouldn't work if the connection was only half open. SYN is used to establish a connection, and an URG is used to prioritize data in a segment.

45. B. In Snort, any value that has ! in front of it is excluded from the rule. For example, `alert tcp !home_net any - > external_net` any alerts on any traffic that is not from the home network that is going out the external network.

46. A. Alternate data streams allow a user to store data in an alternate data stream, which is hidden from most operating system utilities like Windows Explorer, so the secondary files would not appear. Alternate data streams do not allow for any of the other capabilities.

47. D. The Address Resolution Protocol (ARP) is used to resolve IP addresses to MAC addresses. A MAC address is used to communicate at layer 2, which is necessary for communication on the local network. If you were to tell everyone on the network that you owned an IP address and associate that IP address with your MAC address, you would be able to get someone to send you traffic meant for that IP address. None of the other protocols would allow that to happen.

48. D. Dumpster diving is the process of collecting information that an organization carelessly throws away. Some documents contain valuable information, such as bank account statements and even personally identifiable information that should be shredded.

49. C. Tailgating is attempting to blend in with other personnel to enter a secured area. The goal is to trick the security personnel into believing that you are in fact part of the maintenance crew.

50. A. Ransomware is a type of malware that encrypts the operating system. Until the user pays and retrieves the key to decrypt the operating system, they will not have access to their files. In recent years, this has been an increasing threat among users who download files using peer-to-peer applications.

51. A. Server clustering is grouping multiple servers together so they act cooperatively. It provides redundancy, fault tolerance, and improved performance.

52. B. A subject is given a security label called a clearance. Their trustworthiness to process sensitive information determines their level of clearance, such as secret or confidential.

53. C. Monitor mode has to be enabled in order to see radio headers. Promiscuous mode is necessary to see all traffic that comes into an interface, since a network interface filters out all traffic not addressed to the network interface by default. The other modes do not exist.

54. A. Network interfaces filter traffic, only presenting messages addressed to the interface (unicast, broadcast) to the operating system. You can get the interface to forward everything to the operating system if you use promiscuous mode. Monitor mode is used to capture 802.11 traffic. The other modes don't exist.

55. B. The code fragment is SQL, trying to drop a table out of a database by using a semicolon command separator and then the --, which is sometimes used as a comment. As the other attack types do not use SQL, this has to be a SQL injection attack.

56. C. When you have compromised one system and you use it as though it were a router to provide access to systems on networks the compromised system is also on, it's called pivoting. This is because you are moving from the network you compromised the system on to a separate network the target system is also connected to. Piggybacking is a type of physical social engineering attack. Auto-networking is not a thing in this context.

57. A. Secure Copy Protocol (SCP) uses TCP port 22 because it runs over Secure Shell (SSH) and TCP port 22 is the SSH port.

58. A. In order to send a message to someone using asymmetric encryption, you need their public key. This is the only key you would have access to, so it's the key that would be used to encrypt the message. The private key would be used to decrypt the message by the owner of both keys. A symmetric key would not be used to encrypt or decrypt messages in an asymmetric key scenario, and PGP is an example of an implementation of asymmetric encryption.

59. D. In order for an anomaly-based IPS to function properly, a network baseline must be determined. It is recommended to determine the baseline during peak hours and low-usage hours to get a full understanding of behaviors. An anomaly-based IPS does not use rules or signatures.

60. B. In a Fraggle attack, the adversary crafts a packet and pings the broadcast address. The result is that all the nodes within the subnet will respond to the address the adversary forges, causing a DDoS on the victim's computer.

61. B. Slowloris is a tool that was designed to target Solaris web servers. It starved a server by creating multiple TCP sockets, which in turn would cause a DoS for users of the web server.

62. B. Modbus is a protocol that was originally used to communicate using serial interfaces but has been adapted to use network protocols. It is used to interface with industrial control system elements like programmable logic controllers. SCADA is the set of systems that may be used in industrial control systems. While SMTP and SSH may be used in the overall system, they would not commonly be used to communicate with programmable logic controllers.

63. C. Programmable logic controllers are used to control the lowest-level elements in an industrial control system. They may be used to send commands to a production system or to collect data from sensors. The human machine interface is the highest-level element. ICS is an initialism of *industrial control system* and *object* is just a generic word that could mean a lot of things.

64. A. Platform as a Service is a configuration in which the customer can have access to an application server on top of which to build applications. Software as a Service is not used to build applications since the application is already built. FTP is the File Transfer Protocol. A web application may be built on top of Platform as a Service but isn't the computing platform itself.

65. C. Shoulder surfing is used when the adversary is attempting to steal personal information. It is commonly used at automated teller machines to pick up a personal identification number.

66. B. IPv6 has IPSec natively specified as being part of the protocol. This allows security associations to be created between systems, forcing all communications to follow an established policy that may allow encryption or other security controls over that data flow. None of the other protocols supports IPSec natively.

67. D. A proxy is used to capture web requests on a network before being sent on to the specified server. It can be useful for blocking requests to malicious sites as well as monitoring web activity. None of the others would be used to monitor web traffic.

68. B. Classless Inter-Domain Routing (CIDR) is a way of denoting network sizes without needing to write out subnet masks.

69. B. VLANs are separate virtual local area networks that can be used to segregate workstations. This practice can be used to group workstations in a "need to know" network and can prevent others from accessing the network through port security.

70. B. ICMP operates at the layer 3 of the OSI model. ICMP uses echo-request and echo-reply messages to support applications like ping. It is commonly used to diagnose and troubleshoot network connections.

71. C. The easiest way to collect authentication credentials from wireless users is to create an evil twin that will appear to be a legitimate access point in the wireless network they want to connect to. While a deauthentication attack might work, it is not an easy attack. Man in the middle would be hard and wouldn't necessarily work. A rogue access point is on the inside of a network but is unauthorized.

72. A. Address space layout randomization changes the address space, meaning the addresses used by the program, each time the program is run. This means the return address changes every run of the program so manipulating that return address is harder since the attacker doesn't know the address of their code. The stack continues to exist. The return address is not wrapped, and while technically the stack pointer moves in the sense that each run points to a different location, that's not really why buffer overflows are harder on systems that implement address space layout randomization.

73. C. Botnets are groups of computers that a bot herder or a zombie master handler controls. The computers do not necessarily have to be physically located near the master; the master can control the bots via IRC or instant messaging services.

74. D. EternalBlue makes use of vulnerabilities in the implementation of the Server Message Block protocol on Windows systems.

75. D. A Trojan is malicious software appearing to be benign software. While individual Trojan implementations may do each of those things, a Trojan itself does not necessarily. The one thing a Trojan does is pretend to be something it isn't, which means a user may run the Trojan.

76. A. Cain & Abel allows the user to pull passwords from packets in network captures. Wireshark is packet capture software, and while John the Ripper does password cracking, it does not specifically crack passwords from wireless networks. Traceroute is a program used to trace the path a packet would take on its way to a destination.

77. B. The program DIRB can perform brute force attacks against a web server by issuing requests against directory names to see if they exist, regardless of what a web spider may have said. Kismet is a wireless tool, Wireshark is used to capture packets, and setoolkit is used for social engineering.

78. C. While Metasploit is used by setoolkit, Metasploit by itself won't automate a social engineering attack. Setoolkit handles all the automation, making use of exploits available in Metasploit. Nmap is used for port scanning, and Aircrack is a wireless tool.

79. C. Airmon-ng will put an 802.11 card into monitor mode, which is necessary to allow for the capture of radio headers. Nmap is used to scan ports, Ettercap can be used to enable man-in-the-middle attacks, and Ophcrack is used for cracking passwords using rainbow tables.

80. B. The program fping is used for ping sweeps, and it is very efficient at performing them. hping can be used to craft packets. Neither of the other answers is correct.

81. D. A hub is a layer 1 device that broadcasts all the data on all of its ports. Once the adversary gains access to a port, they do not have to do anything other than collect the data.

82. C. A proxy firewall acts as a middleman between the client and the destination server. It will terminate the connection on behalf of the client and can also facilitate packet filtration and conduct stateful inspection.

83. D. With Platform as a Service, the customer is only responsible for all the application elements, which would include application code, any database that supports the application, and any payment processing that may be necessary for the application. The customer is not responsible for the operating system. The provider is responsible for the operating system.

84. C. A digital signature provides non-repudiation, meaning the person who owns the private key that was used to sign the message can't say the message didn't come from them since no one else should have access to use that key. As the message isn't necessarily encrypted, there is no confidentiality. The message doesn't necessarily have a message authentication code like a cryptographic hash to verify integrity, and there is no additional utility that comes from a digital signature.

85. D. In 1978, Ron Rivest, Adi Shamir, and Leonard Adleman proposed using their version of public key cryptography that was far more efficient and more secure than its competitors. Although there were different public key cryptosystems available during that time, they were not as secure as RSA's public key cryptosystem.

86. B. JavaScript Object Notation (JSON) is often used to store and transmit data in a cloud-native design using NoSQL databases. YAML is often used for configuration files but not storing information for an application, though it is self-describing. C is a programming language, as is SQL.

87. C. The regional Internet registries store information about domains, including contact information for the domain. EDGAR is managed by the Securities and Exchange Commission and stores information about public filings for companies. The Domain Name System (DNS) servers wouldn't have contact information about the domain, and LinkedIn wouldn't have that information either, at least not that would be easy to locate.

88. A. TCP is a segment that provides reliable transportation for IP datagrams. A packet is the protocol data unit (PDU) at the network level (IP). A frame is the PDU for layer 2. A nibble is a portion of a byte.

89. B. A remote method invocation (RMI) server is used by Java to provide remote procedure calls and remote object access to applications. You would already know the development language (Java) and couldn't get any information about the developer. Also, you already know what protocols are being used because you found the server and you know it's an RMI server.

90. A. Kerberos is an authentication, accounting, and authorization (AAA) server that uses tickets to grant access to resources. Although it is widely used, it has a few drawbacks, such as using symmetric cryptography and being susceptible to man-in-the-middle attacks. Solaris is an operating environment, Apache is a web server, and Exchange is a collaboration environment.

91. D. A stack pointer is pointed at the top of the memory stack. Memory uses the concept of last in, first out (LIFO), and instructions are either pushed onto the stack or popped off of the stack. Stack frames—the memory blocks that store information like local variables for a function—are pushed onto the stack. Each time a stack frame is pushed on, the stack pointer moves so the next stack frame can be pushed into the right place in memory.

92. C. The macro feature that is found in Apache OpenOffice and in Microsoft Office can be used to execute malicious commands. The macro feature is now disabled by default.

93. B. A signature matches characteristics of a virus. If a polymorphic virus has compromised a system, it would change its signature, making it extremely difficult to detect and eradicate each time it is called.

94. A. Physical control is used to restrict physical access to sensitive equipment, a facility, or an area.

95. A. Vulnerability scanners do not exploit services to determine where there are vulnerabilities. The scanner will gather information from the target and compare that information against a signature that identifies the vulnerability.

96. A. Wardriving is the use of a vehicle like a car to move quickly through a physical space to locate wireless networks. You would need a laptop or other mobile device with Wi-Fi capability in order to identify the wireless networks.

97. D. The command useradd followed by the username is the proper way to add a user.

98. A. The find command will locate a specified file based on the name in the current directory tree given by the user. Because of the intense search effort, it can be slow, but nonetheless, it will almost certainly locate the file.

99. C. Anything that can be executed or retrieved from a target system, including files, configuration settings, or even initiating a network connection to an internal server the target system has access to, is possible using an XML external entity injection. What you can't get is anything on the user side since the XML is being parsed on the server.

100. A. Risks, threats, and vulnerabilities are the three types of assessment that can be used to analyze the current security posture.

101. D. Flood guarding detects flooding and DoS activity and, if tuned properly, reacts in order to disrupt the attack on the network.

102. B. Implicit deny is the default security posture that is set for firewalls. The network administrator must configure the firewall to allow appropriate traffic to enter or leave the network.

103. C. SNMP uses port 161 as the agent, and port 162 is used for management. Port 53 is DNS.

104. B. The Internet Security Association and Key Management Protocol (ISAKMP) is often referred to as the security association manager. It is primarily responsible for managing the agreed method for authentication between two parties.

105. A. WPA2 Enterprise allows for AAA servers such as RADIUS and TACACS to be used. Exchange is a collaboration server that handles mail. NetWare is an old network operating system, and Solaris is an operating environment.

106. C. With spoofing, the adversary intends to falsify information, such as changing the source address of a datagram to the address of the victim, therefore making it difficult to trace the adversary's IP address.

107. D. A web application firewall can be used to look at HTTP traffic to identify potential attacks. Once they have been identified, they may be logged, or the messages may be dropped. A stateful firewall does not look at application-layer traffic. Anti-malware won't look at application messages for web applications. This is also not the job of a load balancer.

108. C. Using LDAP injection, the adversary can craft statements if the front-end web server will accept LDAP query statements. It is best practice to ensure that the server performs sanitization on input values.

109. A. Hopping from one part of the file system to another is called traversing the directory. This tactic is often used if conventional methods such as creating a shell session are not possible.

110. B. Heaps are allocated in a dynamic fashion. Unlike stacks, a heap is generated when an application demands more memory than what was allocated. A stack is used for static information that is known at compile time. There is nothing virtual about this.

111. A. One of the best practices in cyber security is to reduce the surface threat; therefore, it is recommended to disable all ports that are not used by the server.

112. D. The && is a logical operator indicating that if the previous command succeeded, the next one should be run. The command that is next displays the output of the file on a Linux system that contains the password hashes. This is not SQL or XML. Cross-site request forgery happens on the user side.

113. A. Signature identification in Snort is a unique value that represents a particular rule.

114. B. Ferret is a tool that allows a user to capture cookies between systems. Other tools that can facilitate this type of attack are Cain & Abel and Hamster.

115. B. SESAME (Secure European System for Applications in a Multi-vendor Environment) is a authentication, accounting, and authorization server. A user that is requesting access to a server must be authenticated by the authentication server and then request access to the privilege attribute server.

116. D. This operation is a revoke operation under the Take-Grant model. The subject that has the read and write permissions on an object has removed the read permissions. The subject can now only write to the object.

117. A. The final output to the diagram is the digital signature. This diagram depicts an overview of the RSA digital signature generation.

118. A. During the RSA signature verification process, the message is verified by using the results of the signature that is copied. In this case, the user does not need to have the original message in order to determine the integrity of the message.

119. A. When you're XORing, the values that match, such as 0 and 0 or a 1 and a 1, will XOR to a 0. If the values are mismatched, such as 1 and 0 or 0 and 1, then their XOR value will be a 1.

120. C. A monalphabetic cipher, also known as a replacement cipher, exchanges one character for another to complete the encryption and decryption process.

121. D. The BP, or base pointer, is used to reference the local variables in the memory stack.

122. B. On line 8, the ACK is sent back to 23.253.184.229 and is set to 1. This completes the three-way handshake.

123. A. The flag is 0x02, which is "don't fragment."

124. B. Cuckoo Sandbox uses virtualization to allow for execution of a malware sample in isolation. This allows for analysis of the malware sample without the potential for the malware infecting other systems. The strings utility can't be used for dynamic analysis. You could use Ollydbg for dynamic analysis but it wouldn't be safe. The same is true for Cutter.

125. A. The current connection is not vulnerable to Heartbleed because it affects only connections using TLS versions 1.0.1 to 1.0.1f.

Chapter 5: Practice Test 5

1. A. Enumeration is the act of identifying specific services that a target machine is running. It involves connecting to the system, gathering login credentials, and finding open ports and even programs that are installed. Scanning looks for systems, services, and applications. Footprinting is looking for the size of the target, and fingerprinting can be used for different areas.

2. A. Although man-in-the-middle attack may be a possible answer, it does require some sort of interaction on a switch, which is not passive. Sniffing is the correct choice and can be done by using a protocol analyzer such as Wireshark. Password cracking requires you to have password hashes.

3. D. Although complex passwords are great to use, a longer password will maximize the key length in the encryption algorithm. In this case, the longer the password, the more secure it is, even if is a simple password (provided it's not in the dictionary). Ideally, the password would still include symbols and numbers in addition to upper- and lowercase, but the length does make it harder to crack.

4. B. In the directory /var/log, the administrator can access the events that were previously recorded by the operating system.

5. C. The administrator username that Linux defaults to using is root. Best practice to harden a Linux system is to change the default administrator's login to a username other than root. Administrator is the name of the administrative user on Windows. su is a utility on Linux to switch users.

6. A. Port address translation, or PAT, is the method that maps a single IP address to a port that is unique to a web or Internet connection. One IP address can have many port numbers assigned based on connections. None of the others is a real answer.

7. B. The resource identifier (RID) is part of the SID and identifies the user, a domain, or a computer. UID is often short for user identifier. The other two answers are not real.

8. B. Conducting ping sweeps and enumerating a target allow an attacker to get a sense of the scope of the target, meaning how many systems and services there may be in any penetration test. Fingerprinting may be done on operating systems, which requires not just port scans but an analysis of information from the network stack on the target system. Reconnaissance is about gathering information about the target.

9. B. The time that is returned to the user based on the hops the packets takes is recorded in milliseconds. It is usually displayed as *ms* in the terminal. Network communication is fast. Response time measured in seconds or, worse, minutes would be an indication of a very bad network.

10. C. DES has a key space of 64 bits, but 56 bits is the actual key length it uses; the other 8 bits are for parity use.

11. C. The Rijndael algorithm was selected to replace DES. It was renamed the Advanced Encryption Standard (AES) by NIST.

12. C. The ACK flag is sent to the originator of the connection and signifies the establishment of the TCP three-way handshake. The first message is a SYN from the client. The server sends an ACK to the SYN combined with its own SYN, creating a SYN/ACK.

13. D. XOR is exclusive OR, meaning you only get a TRUE if one of the values is TRUE. 1 and 1 would result in a FALSE. A pair of values such as 1 and 0 or 0 and 1 will produce an XOR output of 1.

14. C. Firewalls are used to block traffic into a network, though when you combine a firewall with an intrusion detection system you get an intrusion prevention system that will block traffic based on what has been detected. A packet filtering firewall uses header information, such as source and destination address and port, to determine whether to allow traffic into the network. Syslog and the Windows event subsystem can be used to log system messages. Intrusion detection systems can be used to generate alerts on traffic.

15. A. Google Dorks is a collection of search terms that can be added to by anyone who wants to contribute them and are stored in the website Google Hacking Database. It provides a list of sites that may be vulnerable to SQL injection attacks. Tracert is used to trace the network path between you and a target. 1=1' may be a SQL injection, and there are no Bing hacks.

16. A. The header fields such as source and destination port numbers along with length and checksum have a field length size of 16 bits. This gives a range of values between 0 and 65535, which is the range of port values.

17. B. The value that declares a guess account within Windows has a relative identifier (RID) with a value of 501.

18. C. Ping sweeping the subnet will identify what nodes currently reside on the network. Nodes that are off within that subnet will not respond with an ICMP echo reply. While you can use a port scan, it's not simple, and if you are only scanning ports, you may not get good results if there are no open ports. For this reason, a port scanner like Nmap will initiate a ping before scanning ports to determine if a host is up. A web crawler is used to enumerate pages on a website.

19. D. The Domain Name System uses UDP port 53 for querying and zone transfers. Port 22 is used for SSH. 8080 is an alternate port for web servers, and 80 is the primary port used for web servers that are not using encrypted communication.

20. A. Cain & Abel is a tool that is developed for Windows. Among other things, such as ARP spoofing, Cain & Abel can be used to crack passwords by using the dictionary method or by brute force. Wireshark is used for packet sniffing. ToneLoc is used for war dialing for modems. WarVOX is used for the same purpose.

21. B. The SYN flag initiates the half-open connection. By sending more SYN packets and not responding to any SYN/ACK packets the target sends back, buffer space on the target is consumed. Older systems may end up without the ability to respond because of the consumed resources.

22. D. dig is a tool that is found in Linux systems. It can be used to query information about a server that is hosting DNS services. Twofish is an encryption cipher. Cain & Abel can be used to crack passwords, and WarVOX is used to attack phone systems.

23. B. When you use the alert rule type, the administrator will be notified only if Snort matches the rule to the network traffic. Pass allows traffic through, block is not the right syntax to disallow a packet, and Snort would have to be installed inline for that to work.

24. D. When you use -sT, Nmap will conduct a full TCP connect scan on a host or even a subnet, if required. A SYN scan, also called a half-open scan, is initiated using -sS. You can do a UDP scan using -sU.

25. C. A firewall is a logical control and is often known as a technical control.

26. B. The / indicates that the current user is located in the root directory when they operating in a Linux environment. C:\ is the root of the primary disk by default in Windows installations. The backslash, \, is an escape character and not used in the names of files or directories on Linux systems.

27. A. Pretending to be a trusted person to a user is a pretext and is a common social engineering attack technique. Tailgating is a physical social engineering attack. The technique described in the question is neither piggybacking nor masquerading.

28. D. Driving around to pick up open wireless access points is called wardriving. There are many tools that can be used for this type of attack. While buildings have sometimes been marked with chalk, it's not called warchalking. War dialing is used to attack phone-based network connections.

29. C. ARP poisoning is when the adversary injects their own MAC address onto the network in order to sniff traffic on the LAN. Reverse ARP is used to acquire an IP address using just its media access control (MAC) address and is considered an obsolete protocol.

30. C. Lambda functions are serverless, meaning there is no server that is being instantiated to support the function that the developer or operations staff has to do anything with. As far as they are concerned, there is no server. While it's possible the application is also service-oriented, there is not enough information to make that determination. These are virtualized functions, but the application isn't virtualized.

31. A. A keylogger, which can be a hardware or software solution, records the input that is generated from the user. Most often, the input that is received is either recorded locally to the device or transmitted back to the owner of the keylogger. There is no key scanner in this context. Neither a rootkit nor a Trojan is necessarily going to collect information like that referenced here.

32. D. Using ifconfig in Linux will display wireless adapters and Ethernet devices that are currently installed on the workstation. The command ipconfig is used on Windows workstations. It is used to get directory listings, and netstat is used to show network statistics.

33. B. The /bin directory contains the basic commands Linux utilizes. The /etc directory is used to hold configuration settings. The / directory is the root of the entire file system.

34. C. Piggybacking is the act of trying to blend in with the crowd in order to circumvent security measures. In this case, the attacker is using boxes to play on the kindness of people to gain easy access to a facility. There is no sliding or simming, and phishing is an attack type that uses email.

35. B. Cookies are text files that contain information about your connection to a web server. They can hold authentication and session details. An HTML file holds the source for static web pages. An XML file may store configuration or data associated with the application. A text file could store anything, but cookies are not commonly stored in text files.

36. D. An adversary who records open access points by marking their location on buildings nearby is engaging in warchalking. This signifies to others that there is an open access point to use. Wardriving is the process of driving around an area to locate wireless networks. Foot-printing is the acquisition of information about a target to get a sense of the size and scope.

37. B. Metamorphic viruses change themselves every time they infect a file. For the most part, metamorphic viruses are difficult to detect with antivirus software because they constantly change their signature. Polymorphic viruses change the way they look but may not rewrite themselves or have the ability to make changes themselves. A Trojan doesn't necessarily have the ability to rewrite itself, nor does a shell virus.

38. D. SHA-1 was developed by the NSA, and it was soon apparent that it had flaws. In 2005, the U.S. government made an effort to replace it due to its flaws. MD5 only has 128 bits of output. HAVAL is an older hashing algorithm but was not developed by the NSA, even if it could generate 160 bits of output. DSA is not a hashing algorithm

39. A. Port 8080 is an alternative to using port 80 for web servers. Port 21 is one of the ports used for FTP. Port 110 is used for POP3 and port 54 is used for a Xerox protocol.

40. A. Using -T 0 is considered the paranoid scan, which is the slowest scan possible to evade detection. -T 5 is the fastest scan. -sX initiates an XMAS scan and -sT performs a full-connect scan.

41. A. Wireshark is an application that can inspect both wireless and Ethernet packets. Aircrack is an older tool used against wireless networks, Cain & Abel is used for password gathering and Nmap is used for port scanning.

42. B. Cloudscan is used to assess cloud services. Samba is a network sharing application based around the Server Message Block protocol. Postman is an application used to test web application programming interfaces. Nmap is a port scanner that could be used to identify any devices on a network as well as the ports open on a device.

43. D. An administrator would use the command passwd followed by the username, which is user. The system will then prompt for the password. The chmod command is used to set permissions on files and directories. None of the other commands are valid on a Linux system.

44. B. Using arp -a will display the current ARP cache that the workstation is holding. The ifconfig and ipconfig commands are used to get configuration information for the network interfaces on a system.

45. C. nslookup is an application that provides information about a server that uses DNS. It can also show who made the zone transfer and when it occurred. Cain & Abel is used to gather passwords. ICMP is a protocol, not an application, and you are using nslookup against the Domain Name Service (DNS) server.

46. B. Top-level domains are designated by .com, .net, .org, and even .gov, to name a few. They are also known as top-level domains. myserver.com includes the domain name, and the other two are URLs and not domains.

47. D. Scanning is the second phase of the hacking methodology, followed by maintaining access and ending with covering your tracks.

48. C. Public key infrastructure, or PKI, uses certificate authorities to sign certificates and issue them to subjects.

49. A. NIST uses `http://nvd.nist.gov` to publish the latest vulnerabilities for public knowledge. Google is a good search engine but doesn't store a database of vulnerabilities. Neither of the other sites is valid.

50. C. Competitive intelligence is the process of using your competitor's information to your advantage. Products that the competitor has on the market may be used for analysis and even reverse engineering.

51. C. SNMPv1 transported community strings as a method of authentication through plain text. Because hackers were able to use SNMPv1 to exploit nodes, it was later upgraded to version 2 and then later version 3 in which the community strings are now encrypted. Telnet is a client, server, and protocol used to interact remotely with systems. SFTP is used to transfer files using encryption to protect the contents.

52. A. RADIUS is an authentication, authorization, and accounting server that is used to facilitate an enterprise solution for access control. In this case, WPA2 Enterprise will use RADIUS as a means to provide a secure service to its users.

53. B. When separation of duties is enforced, one subject cannot accomplish a specific task without the other. The intent is to prevent collusion and maintain the integrity of that specific task.

54. C. A vulnerability is a weakness in a system or application that can be exploited. If a vulnerability exists, it means that there is a threat that can be exploited. A threat vector is the path a threat uses to compromise a system. Malware is malicious software, and threat surface is the entire exposure to threats a system or network has.

55. C. HTTP, the protocol used to transfer web-based communications, is stateless. This makes it hard for applications to maintain an understanding of where they are in any transaction. Because of that, representational state transfer (REST) applications are commonly used. REST is not mandated by RFC.

56. D. The client must have the SSID in order to be associated to an access point. Association to an access point is not authentication; the user must have the password to be authenticated to the access point. Once the SSID is known, the station can attempt to authenticate. This authentication may take many forms, including username and password, but the station has to know what SSID to connect to.

57. C. While you can capture traditional traffic using promiscuous mode, to get the radio traffic, you need to have your wireless network interface set to monitor mode.

58. D. Using `rm` as the command will remove a file from the directory. To remove files and folders recursively, the command is `rm -r`.

59. A. A digital signature on an email is proof that it came from the original sender. Using asymmetric encryption such as Digital Signature Authority (DSA) and RSA are methods to provide nonrepudiation for emails.

60. D. Software as a Service and Storage as a Service gives the customer the least responsibility. This is followed by Platform as a Service and then finally Infrastructure as a Service, which has the most responsibility in the hands of the customer.

61. B. A rootkit is a type of malware that may provide the adversary with a backdoor entrance to the compromised system. A Trojan is a piece of malware that appears to be benign but is in fact malicious. Spyware is used to gather information from a target system.

62. B. Metasploit is a framework that can be used in many different scenarios to compromise a system and user accounts. Cain & Abel is used to collect passwords. Ettercap is used for man-in-the-middle attacks.

63. C. Using `net use` followed by `ipc$ "" /u: ""` will set up a null session with your target. It can be used in part with password sniffing efforts. Netcat can be used to initiate network connections to other systems but isn't used for null sessions. FTP is used to transfer files but does not use that format for initiating connections if you are using the command-line client.

64. C. Base64 encoding is used to change binary code into the ASCII format. It can be used to circumvent firewalls and IDSs. While you can get an ASCII string from a hash algorithm like MD5 and SHA-1, they are not reversible. A binary file can't just be converted to XML, and there is no ASCII version 2.

65. A. Spear phishing targets users that may have specific information an attacker is looking for. Whaling is targeting big "phish" who would commonly be executives. There may be theft going on but the specific technique in use here is a phishing message.

66. A. AirCheck is a commercial product that can be used to check for wireless networks. None of the other answers are used for testing for wireless networks.

67. C. The `-T4` switch allows the user to scan a node or a network in a fast manner. `-oX` is used to generate XML output and `-sS` is used to initiate a SYN scan.

68. A. The URG flag is used to indicate there is priority data in the packet. The receiving station would then refer to the URG pointer, which indicates the offset of the urgent message in the packet.

69. B. A /25 indicates that the user is scanning a subnet that hosts 126 nodes. The /25 indicates there are 25 bits of the 32-bit IP address used for the network address, leaving 7 bits for the host. 2^7 is 128 with possible values of 0–127.

70. C. The user would most likely be using Google. Google allows special keywords to look for specific information. There is a website that keeps track of a lot of these search terms called the Google Hacking Database since the use of these special keywords is called Google Hacking.

71. B. The supervisor can force an employee to take a mandatory vacation. This allows the supervisor to see if fraudulent activities still occur.

72. C. Using the public key of the receiver guarantees that the information that the sender submits cannot be open by anyone other than the receiver, who can decrypt it with his private key.

73. B. A PTR record indicates that the IP address is mapped to a hostname. MX records are used to identify mail server (exchanger) systems. NS records are for name servers, and CNAME records are canonical names or aliases mapping one hostname to another hostname.

74. A. Firewalking is a reconnaissance type of action that determines ports that are open through a firewall.

75. D. Malware that locks the user from their device and demands payment in exchange for the key is ransomware. It uses cryptographic software to encrypt the device, preventing the user from accessing it.

76. A. Bluesnarfing is an attack on a mobile device using Bluetooth, where information can be stolen from the victim's device. Bluejacking is using Bluetooth to send messages to a victim's phone.

77. A. Anything that is publicly available, such as the contents of a newspaper, is consider open-source information.

78. C. Smishing is the use of SMS or text messages to get a victim to do something they wouldn't normally do, including visiting foreign or suspicious websites. Vishing is using voice calls to elicit information from the victim. Whaling is phishing very important or high-value targets, and spear phishing is phishing in a very targeted way.

79. A. Increasing the time rate will force the DNS server to update the DNS cache. This will reduce the likelihood of users becoming victims of site redirection attacks and other DNS poisoning activities.

80. A. Using `filetype:` in Google will search for websites that contain the file type specified after `filetype`. For example, `filetype:pdf` will search for PDF files. The keyword `inurl` searches for content in a URL or web address. The other two answers are not valid Google hacking keywords.

81. B. The SHA-1 algorithm produces an output value of 160 bits. MD5 produces a 128-bit value. SHA-256 generates 256-bit values, and Diffie-Hellman is a key exchange algorithm and not a hashing algorithm.

82. A. The X.509 is the digital certificate standard that is used with certificate authorities. 802.1X is an authentication standard for wired connections. PKI is public key infrastructure and not a format. X.500 is the directory specification that X.509 falls under.

83. C. Asymmetric encryption uses a public and private key that are mathematically related. No other keys can be used with the two that are related.

84. A. The public key is available on the certificate so users can communicate with the subject in a secure manner.

85. C. The attacker likely installed a keylogger, which records every key that was pressed on the system. While you may have virus that is a keylogger, there is a specific type of software called a keylogger. A keylogger is also a type of malware, but specifically, this is talking about the keylogger software. There is no key retriever.

86. A. Because an ACK scan will generate a RST message for both open and closed ports, only ports that have been blocked by a firewall will yield no result, indicating the port is being blocked. The other scans will get different results for open and closed, making it easier to determine whether ports are open but harder to be sure about firewall rules.

87. A. POP3 uses port 110 for email services. Port 53 is used for DNS, 443 is used for encrypted web communications, and port 125 is not a commonly used port.

88. A. When you use automation, you can get consistency, because automation is performed by scripts that will always execute the same way every time. This will also get you repeatability. Because they are scripts, you can test them. What you don't necessarily get is fault tolerance.

89. C. A behavior-based IDS can alert when there is abnormal activity being conducted on the network. In order for the IDS to be effective, a baseline must be set during peak and off-peak times.

90. B. ARP poisoning the default gateway will cause you to receive all the traffic on the network. Proceed with caution, however, because if your workstation does not have enough processing power and there is high network activity, you can potentially cause a DoS on the network.

91. D. No matter where you are, security controls are essential. While cloud providers have all the same controls (or enhanced in many cases) as those you have on-premise, you may not have in-house expertise to be able to implement those controls since they use different technologies. All of the other answers would be the same whether you were on-premise or in the cloud.

92. C. SESAME uses asymmetric encryption as a secured method of authentication. Kerberos provides only symmetric encryption. FTP is the File Transfer Protocol, and RADIUS doesn't support asymmetric encryption.

93. C. Wireshark can be used to monitor and capture network activity. Metastploit is an attack framework, and Netcraft is a website that keeps track of website statistics. Nmap is a port scanner.

94. B. Port 21 is the command port for FTP. This port allows for arbitrary commands to be received from the user. Port 22 is used for SSH, port 20 is used for data transmission for FTP, and port 23 is used for Telnet.

95. D. Files are not objects that Active Directory utilizes. Files are stored within the file system. Active Directory is used to manage system resources like users, computers, and printers.

96. A. Setoolkit is a tool that uses Metasploit and allows the user to spoof social media websites and even craft spear phishing emails. Ettercap is used to perform poisoning attacks to intercept traffic, Mimikatz is used to collect passwords, and netcat is used to connect to network services manually.

97. B. Peach is a fuzzing tool, which can be used to send arbitrary and anomalous data to applications. This data may cause crashes, which might result in the discovery of previously unidentified vulnerabilities. Nmap is a port scanning tool. Mimikatz is used to gather passwords, and Rubeus is a tool that can be used to perform Kerberoasting attacks.

98. A. ICMP Type 3, Code 3 is "destination unreachable, port unreachable," which indicates that the client is down.

99. B. In the OSI model and the TCP/IP model, the Transport layer remains the same.

100. A. The Data Link layer encapsulates the header and trailer of a packet.

101. B. Traceroute can be used to determine if a firewall appliance is being used. If traceroute stops returning results before the trace reaches its destination, it may indicate that a firewall is being used along the path. Metasploit is an exploit framework. Both nslookup and dig are used to gather information from DNS servers.

102. B. A NULL scan will not provide a response if the port is opened on the distant end. An XMAS scan sets the FIN, PUSH, and URG flags. A half-open scan is a SYN scan, and an ACK scan sets the ACK flag.

103. A. One method of fingerprinting a machine to identify the operating system running on the target system is to conduct a port scan. This will generate enough information about the network stack on the target that a tool like nmap can identify the operating system.

104. A. The SRV record is used to advertise services based on the hostname and the ports of the server. A PTR record maps an IP address to a hostname, while an A record maps a hostname to an IP address. There is no SVR record in DNS.

105. D. The SYN packet initiates the TCP connection. There are no hello or broadcast packets in TCP. An ACK is the response to a SYN message.

106. B. The serial number is a unique value that identifies the certificate that is provided by the certificate authority.

107. C. RSA uses two large numbers that are factored together as its basis for encryption. It is used to create digital signatures and symmetric key exchange.

108. A. A SID of 500 is the first administrator's account. The SID of each additional account created will increase by 1.

109. B. Covering your tracks is the process of deleting and altering log files and users' names so that the victim is unable to identify the hacker.

110. B. The /etc/passwd file is used to store administrative information about a user such as their name, phone number, and office number. The /etc/shadow file contains password hashes. /home is a directory, not a file.

111. A. UDP port 137 provides name services with NetBIOS.

112. C. The alert rule type will create a log and alert the administrator if a packet matches the specified rule in Snort.

113. B. Modbus is a protocol developed for serial communications to devices like programmable logic controllers and used by ICS/SCADA infrastructure. XML is not a protocol. While SNMP or SMTP may be used by ICS/SCADA systems, they are not associated as closely as Modbus and weren't developed for serial communications.

114. B. Netstat provides the user with information on what connections are currently active on the client. It also provides the IP address and what state the connection is in, such as listening or established.

115. B. As shown in the bottom of the packet, it is annotated that the flags set are A and F for ACK and FIN, and their value is set using 1.

116. A. The destination port that is used in the current TLS connection is 51738.

117. C. Using netstat, the computer has an established connection coming from stackoverflow web server on TCP port 52017.

118. D. The TTL value is 57.

119. C. In traceroute, an indication that a user encountered a firewall is annotated by the ***. In this example, the firewall occurred at hop 15.

120. C. In the first hop, 192.168.1.1 is the source for the traceroute request.

121. A. The client will receive the server's authentication to be granted access to the requested services.

122. A. Raeleah has both read and execute permissions for Object 3 in the access control list.

123. C. In the bottom section of the packet, the value that is displayed in plain text shows that the user is using Mozilla Firefox as their browser.

124. A. The alias record is annotated by the CNAME record type. In this case, rayojo.tripod .com is the alias that falls under the members.tripod.com zone.

125. A. The SSID that is using the highest channel is Rokugan5.

Index

Comprehensive Online Learning Environment

Register to gain one year of FREE access to the Sybex online interactive learning environment and test bank to help you study for your Certified Ethical Hacker (CEH v11) certification exam—included with your purchase of this book!

Register and Access the Online Test Bank

To register your book and get access to the online test bank, follow these steps:

1. Go to www.wiley.com/go/sybextestprep.
2. Select your book from the list.
3. Complete the required registration information, including answering the security verification to prove book ownership. You will be emailed a PIN code.
4. Follow the directions in the email or go to www.wiley.com/go/sybextestprep. Find your book in the list there and click Register Or Login.
5. Enter the PIN code you received and click the Activate button.
6. On the Create an Account or Login page, enter your username and password, and click Login or create a new account. A success message will appear.
7. Once you are logged in, you will see the online testbank you have registered and should click the Go To Test Bank button to begin.

Do you need more practice? If you have not already read Sybex's *CEH v11: Certified Ethical Hacker Version 11 Study Guide* by Ric Messier (ISBN: 978-1-119-80028-6) and are not seeing passing grades on these practice tests, that book is an excellent resource to master the CEH topics. The Study Guide series maps every exam objective to the corresponding chapter in the book to help track exam prep objective by objective, includes challenging review questions in each chapter to prepare for exam day, and offers online prep materials with flashcards and additional practice tests.